For Adrian
St Louis, October.

Winning the Dust Bowl

from
Carter Revard

Volume 47

SUN TRACKS
An American Indian Literary Series

SERIES EDITOR
Ofelia Zepeda

EDITORIAL COMMITTEE
Vine Deloria, Jr.
Larry Evers
Joy Harjo
Geary Hobson
N. Scott Momaday
Irvin Morris
Simon J. Ortiz
Emory Sekaquaptewa
Kate Shanley
Leslie Marmon Silko
Luci Tapahonso

For all the families and all our relations

Contents

Illustrations

Unless otherwise indicated, photographs are from collections of members of Carter Revard's families. The author is grateful to members of his Osage and Ponca families who have lent these to him and permitted them to be reproduced here.

Osage and Ponca Family Members

following page 38

Jacob Jump (Osage grandfather), c. 1910–15
Jacob, Josephine, Addison, and Louis Jump, c. 1917–18
Arita Jump (aunt), c. 1932–33
Addison, Thelma, and Ireta Jump, c. 1934–35
Students at the Chilocco Indian School, 1948, including Ireta Jump
Louis James Jump (brother), on his way to Korea, 1955
Aunt Jewell McDonald, c. 1929
McDonald family, White Eagle, Oklahoma, c. 1904–5
Ponca relatives, 1990
Cousins Dwain and Craig Camp with Eagle Staff, 1991

Irish, Scotch-Irish, Osage, and Ponca Family Members at Buck Creek, Oklahoma

following page 138

Thelma Camp, 1923 (age 15)
Uncle Aubrey, Loretta, and Roy Camp, c. 1928

To The Reader

This book tells of growing up in a mixed-blood family of Indian and Irish and Scotch-Irish folks, and names some of those who have helped me redeem the time I was given. It moves from Oklahoma to Oxford and the Isle of Skye, to Jerusalem, Paris, and the Isle of Patmos, to Knossos, Bellagio, St. Louis, Cahokia Mounds, and California. There are stories of Poncas and Osages, of the American Indian Movement and urban Indian centers. Some are powwow stories, some Oxford fables; some talk of racing greyhounds and stealing watermelons, others of bootlegging and bankrobbing. As for kissing, there's no telling: where I come from, paparazzi rhymes with Nazi.

I've made this a home of new and selected poems, and put a meadow around it of history and autobiography, by looking out from the poems at the people, places, and happenings from 1931 to the present. The "selected" poems are mostly not taken from *An Eagle Nation* but from *Ponca War Dancers* or *Cowboys and Indians, Christmas Shopping*. Some are "new"—or published only in journals or anthologies. Most of them tell of transformations and awaken-ings, of coming into new beings and understandings, greeting the world and our relatives in a good way. They are not set in chrono-logical order—instead, "earlier" and "later" poems are placed near each other like angled mirrors, so that full-face, profile, and rear-view versions of their subjects may be seen together. Whether pos-terity will stamp these for passport into its undiscovered country a few hundred years may decide; to its Customs Agents I have nothing to declare but such handmade goods, to be given away wherever they might be wanted.

All of the prose settings were newly written for this book. I wrote them down because, at readings, people would ask how certain poems grew as they did, and why in those particular forms—so I would talk of how Coyote came into a sonnet, how greyhound racing was origami-folded into a sestina, why a Birch Canoe spoke Anglo-Saxon, why walking on the Isle of Skye brought me out of blank verse into free verse. Facing that last question, I saw that a real change of "style" comes from a real change in "life"—that is, in how I am related to the world that lives in and around me, and how I use language to deal with it. Seeing this makes me think no questions are small, they simply reduce and expand themselves to suit the mind that entertains them—oak down to acorn, seed up to sequoia. Giving the poems their stories has let me hear better the beings in whom each piece began. And since past listeners have liked the stories, I hope future readers may. I hope they will like also the old photographs of people alive in these stories, which the University of Arizona Press have let me include.

Let me say something about experiences that are not played up a lot in this book. I've been paid a dollar a day to cut up cows bloated and beginning to stink, dead for two or three days—skinning, gutting, disjointing and slicing them up for greyhounds to eat. I've gone to school raggedy and ashamed of myself and the lard-can of navy beans my folks fixed us for lunch, and I've watched a fair amount of rough stuff with whisky and beer, and stood around in grocery stores while my mother was asking the owner to hold off until the end of the month before cashing the check she handed him, and watched his face as he decided to take the check that he knew was not going to clear even then. Over a span of years in Buck Creek I've watched the deputies come for my uncles, have put up bail money for relatives, with Ponca AIM cousins in White Eagle hit the floor while car-lights of what may have been a drive-by shooting moved slowly past—and ours was one of the less tough situations in that Depression-then-War-then-AIM time and Oklahoma place. In short, I grew up poor in a mixedblood family on a reservation among people like ourselves, trying to resist and survive the incoming flak from people who thought they were not like ourselves, hitting us with loud or silent messages that everything happening to us was our fault. But while some poems in this collection speak directly from that foxhole, most assume and celebrate a temporary survival, though the war has no end. One way to survive is to keep a sense of hope, of being able to find what works, what helps, the laughter and shared strength and awareness of good things and good ways. A lot of the poems in this book look "on the bright side," in that hopeful direction—this water's too muddy to drink, but it does hold a star. In Hell, as Milton put it, "hope never comes, that comes to all," but it did come to Oklahoma, and a lot of this book tells of its visiting now and then (not only in Oklahoma, of course) like a hummingbird that shows us where spring flowers are—and where, with its pollination, the summer's fruits will be.

Watching a rubythroat taste the blue morning glories by our kitchen window, I used to wonder how it might be to live like a hummingbird—on the sweets of life, just touching the world on its blossoms, taking only what's meant to be taken, at every touch bringing out new lives, perching unharmed on lightning-filled wires to look down into this world, then before all the North's flowers have fallen, go humming over the Gulf of Mexico to the nectar of southern blossoms. Now, it would seem almost as good to speak or write so that an iridescence of words might fly out to visit other minds in those ways, to make poems that befriend readers, bring fruits of understanding. As humans we need all the friends we can find, being social creatures in a world of strangers, and sometimes the only place to find them is a solitary room with a book or two. Not every friendship comes alive at first sight, but over time the things friends say and mean become clearer, are understood better— and if any of these poems reach friends, I hope that is how things will go for each reader and his or her significant other.

There is no way I can make these pieces as beautiful and useful as hummingbirds, though maybe plain human awkwardness will have its uses. Yet if they don't help readers to laugh and cry, under- stand, wonder, and be surprised by ordinary beings, they are not poems. If they are needed, if they do these things, if they touch readers at the heart, then readers will get them by heart, and keep them alive in that place where although time erodes it makes a grand canyon, a history of earth with the water of life running through. For my part I hope it is true that good language, in both talk and writing, builds a small community in which people can live a little more completely and joyously than solitude allows—words are not poems until that happens. Poetry is not just about what is unique to an author, an "I," it is mostly about what is shared, what is common to author and readers. It is not so helpful as good carpentry, or plumbing, or farming, or parenting, but is of some use when well and truly done. If these poems meet that standard, they will find their readers.

I could have omitted much that is here, or I could have stuffed in more stories, and I might have relocated all the pieces in a chronological sequence—but I chose not to stay on that hypnotic Interstate. There are (I think) good reasons why the numbered "chapters" precede and follow each other as they do, and I'll not object if good listeners catch some harmonies and counterpoints—but had I enclosed other poems, and notes or comments to go with them, a wilder music might have let us meet different scenes and beings. This is an abridgment of one life and some of its letters—not a finished tome, but a little night music that could be re-sequenced, cut, or extended and re-shaped. In this it follows the planless plan of Mark Twain in composing his *Autobiography*—if only I could write it half so well.

As for prose cadences and rhythms, there are a few writers besides Twain whose late-night windows I like to walk past as friend: John Joseph Mathews, Benjamin DeMott, Tom Wolfe, Stanley Elkin, and William Gass. They'll be horrified to hear it, but Jo Mathews gave me Osage country; Ben DeMott showed me there could be a decent Harvard; I saw that the red dust of Oklahoma back roads may settle naturally onto the tangerine-flake prose of Tom Wolfe; Stanley opened the inexhaustible cornucopia of English grammar; and Bill Gass donated the well-tempered clavier once played by Peter Quince.

Winning the Dust Bowl

Finding a Voice

Thinking about the fragile greatness of Imperial America, I tried to recall how I found a voice to speak in this great wilderness. Where I found it was in Oklahoma, Land of the Red People, and it was Coyote who gave this voice; so on public occasions it seems good to begin with the words in which he first showed me how the sounds of the world turn into music:

Coyote Tells Why He Sings

There was a little rill of water, near the den,
That showed a trickle, all the dry summer
When I was born. One night in late August, it rained—
The Thunder waked us. Drops came crashing down
In dust, on stiff blackjack leaves, on lichened rocks,
And the rain came in a pelting rush down over the hill,
Wind blew wet into our cave as I heard the sounds
Of leaf-drip, rustling of soggy branches in gusts of wind.

And then the rill's tune changed—I heard a rock drop
That set new ripples gurgling, in a lower key.
Where the new ripples were, I drank, next morning,
Fresh muddy water that set my teeth on edge.
I thought how delicate that rock's poise was and how
The storm made music, when it changed my world.

That sonnet was written in Amherst, Massachusetts, upstairs
in the old Mabel Loomis Todd house where I was living in 1957–58.
(That's the house where Mrs. Todd, wife of the Amherst College
astronomer, used to hold her trysts with Emily Dickinson's brother,
Austin, the treasurer of Amherst College. Or, to put it in rhyme, it's
where Austin and Mabel did it on the table.) I was then teaching at
Amherst College, after getting back from Oxford and out of Yale,
and one morning before dawn I woke up to the sound of rain on the
roof. A hint of light was just beginning to grow outside the window,
the kind Tennyson had in mind in "Tears, Idle Tears":

Ah, sad and strange as in dark summer dawns
The earliest pipe of half-awakened birds
To dying ears, when unto dying eyes
The casement slowly grows a glimmering square;
So sad, so strange, the days that are no more.

But this was a wintry not a summery dawn, and the rain on the
roof had a duller sound than that of big summer drops. And yet
there were *all kinds* of rain-sounds coming in there to that second-
floor bedroom under the eaves—the tap and splash on roof and
window, the tankatoonkatinktinktonky gurgle of the gutter's tin, the
swish and plish and creak of twig and branch in an elm, the sizzly
plop and splish of drops on grass, the whispering silk of rain caress-
ing wind. It would have made John Cage envious, those four
minutes and forty-four seconds I lay there listening while Nobody
played that wonderful piano.

And then a terrible thought struck me: I was going deaf, and
before long would not hear again the sound of rain before dawn. Six
years earlier a doctor had tapped a tuning fork and held it beside my
right ear till I no longer heard it hum; then he put its base against
the back of my skull—and I heard that silvery steel for twenty seconds more. This meant I had otosclerosis, a kind of hereditary
arthritis of the ear's little bones—the prognosis being that in a few
years I would be as deaf as my mother and my Uncle Arthur.

For some years, it's true, I kept my wonderful bone-conduction hearing—when I held up a ticking watch to my ear, I could not hear it, but when I put it against my right elbow the TICKaTICK-TICKyTICK was there in high-digital clarity and detail. I had always loved hearing birds before dawn: now it seemed unlikely that a bluebird would come and perch on my right elbow to sing, as the sun came up, *O Sóle Mio*.

Those were not happy thoughts, there in the Amherst dawn; so for a little while I took Queen Victoria's advice—lay back and thought of England: that is, I recited those Tennysonian lines about how sad and strange it was, unto dying ears and all. Then something in the swash of wind and rain against the window struck a different note—and there flashed to mind an Oklahoma thunderstorm that had once caught us, my brothers and sisters and me, when we had walked one day up to what we called the Big Rocks, up out of our bluestem meadow and across Doe Creek to the great boulders falling gradually down from the wooded rim of the hills to the northwest of us. They were twenty, thirty, forty feet high, with chasms and mini-canyons among them full of dead leaves with centipedes and scorpions and lizards and rattlesnakes, and you could climb up along their eroded knobbly sides to a slanting or level top, hide among oak and ash and hickory leaves, and look down on any travelers you intended to ambush and rob.

But of course we were the only travelers, though we could read the names of those who had climbed there many years before and scratched or cut their names into the soft sandstone with forty- or fifty-year-old dates from the 1890s and early 1900s, when these were still unallotted lands of the Osage Reservation, wooded hills of Indian Territory where outlaws hid from the Kansas or Missouri or U.S. marshals, their only worry being whether a band of Osage tribal police might ride up and roust them off the Reservation, or whether a U.S. marshal—maybe my great-uncle Franklin Revard, later a member of the Osage Tribal Council—might get the drop on them and take them back to jail in Pawhuska to hold for trial. Half the names on these boulders, though, were set into hearts carved there by courting couples who used to ride out on horseback or in buggies from Bartlesville, the little trading post of Jake Bartles five miles to the east and just outside the Reservation, where the first oil in Oklahoma would be discovered and Frank Phillips would found Phillips Petroleum, whose headquarters are still in Bartlesville.

It was one time when we were reading those names that the thunderstorm came up from the southwest, and we saw it coming but dawdled, hoping it would sweep past over the hills to the west of us. As we watched though, the wall clouds came swirling and spitting lightning toward us, and just as the first lines of rain swept over us we scrambled down off the rocks and ran stooping into a shelter, almost a cave, its hollow slanting down and back to a dark crevice with suspiciously musky smells—coyote or bobcat we thought, more likely skunk. But the storm drowned that worry as the big drops began slamming down on the leaves and rocks and the deep hot dust below.

It was that slashing and swashing downpour, that blinding cloudburst of roar and grumble, that I suddenly remembered there in my Amherst bed, and I said in surprise: suppose there *was* a den of coyotes there, and the pups were just opening their eyes, what would that thunderstorm have sounded like to them, given the wonderful ears a coyote has? And then I thought of hearing the coyotes singing, of a moonlight night, from the hills north and west of our valley, there by the Big Rocks, and I said, maybe that's *why* they sing. So I got out of bed, about five-thirty, and started trying to write what the coyote child would have heard and said.

By 8:00 A.M., when I had to go and teach my classes, I had thirteen lines. Then I had to hold conferences and go to departmental meetings, and when I finally got home at 6:00 that evening I looked at the page and said Hmmn, thirteen lines—one more and I've got a sonnet. Pretty soon, after a couple more hours, the fourteenth line showed up, and it turned out to be what the whole poem was about.

Much later, when Joseph Bruchac interviewed me for the collection of essays he was doing for the University of Arizona Press (*Survival This Way*, 1987), he reminded me that in the sonnet Coyote says, "The Thunder waked me," and since Joe knew that at my naming ceremony I had been brought into the Thunder clan, he asked me if I was thinking of that when I wrote the poem. I told him I did not consciously mean to make that connection, but realized soon after that I had done so. So Coyote came and gave me my voice, and maybe the Thunder had come to give him his, and now we try to make from all the sounds of the world a music worth singing to the moon.

2

Inviting the Muse to Oklahoma

But once the voice has come, a song is wanted, so you ask the Music
to come down where words might be found to go along with it.
Aganippe Well is what Sir Philip Sidney called one of the Muses'
springs on Mount Helicon—the lower one (the upper one,
Hippocrene, where the great winged horse Pegasus touched down,
is only for epic poetry). In 1975 Stella and I, on a trip to Greece
with three kids, drove up and down the mountains in a Volkswagen,
and we drank from the springs of Aphrodite, Hermes, Zeus, and
assorted other gods and muses.

    Remembering, back in St. Louis, those mountain springs in
Greece, my mind went back again to the dry blackjack hills around
the Buck Creek Valley, and I remembered that there were small
springs up there, and how in one of the hot summers of the Dust
Bowl times we had to truck some barrels up into those hills to a
spring and fill them there, so we could drink, and cook. I thought
how, even then, there was a little water in the pond my folks had
made for the cows and horses, where they managed to drink, even in
the cold winters, once we had chopped a hole in the ice. To see
them so thirsty, and to help them quench that thirst, in a parched
summer or a frozen winter, that was how I remembered those hot
dry Grecian mountains with their Muses' springs. Not just for
word-slingers, but for all who need water, that's why the Muses
come down. So I cut open a piece I had written about the pond, and
invited the Muses and the Thunder to come in and stay for a spell.
As I say, in the hills around Buck Creek there are some springs, but

on the meadow where I grew up we had to build a place for what
the heavens sent down, and then the Muses came.

But you know, the cow-pond we dug and dammed in
Oklahoma had the advantage that you could swim in it, in the
company of various other more than human creatures. When my
Grandfather Camp used to ride Beauty, our half-Arabian pinto
mare, down for a drink in the pond he had made, she would first
wade in a little, put her head down and take a long drink, but when
his attention wandered would surge out deeper, lie down, and roll
over in the cooling waters, thus evoking from him some remarkable
poetry. Which may go to show that before you bridle a Muse, you
should learn to swim. Anyway, I call this piece, which looks to me
like a Grecian urn on the page,

To the Muse, in Oklahoma

That *Aganippe Well* was nice, it hit the spot—
sure, this bluestem meadow
is hardly Helicon, we had
to gouge a pond, the mules
dragged a rusty slip scraping
down through dusty topsoil into
dark ooze and muck, grating open
sandstone eggs; but then the thunder
sent living waters down, they filled
the rawness with blue trembling where white
clouds sailed in summer and we
walked upon the water
every winter (truth's
a zero allomorph of time), although
it was more fun sliding. We'd go and
chop down through six-inch ice by
the pond's edge, pry the
ice-slab out onto the pond from its
hole where the dark water welled
up cold to the milk-cows sucking noisily,
snorting their relish—and when

they'd drunk, we shoved the ice-
slab over to where the bank
sloped gently, took
a running chute and leaped atop the slab real
easy and slid,
        just glided clear over
the pond, riding on ice. Or we stretched prone
on the black windowy ice,
looked down on darkness where fish
drifted, untouchable, below our fingers.
Ice
        makes a whole new surface
                        within things, keeps
killer whales from seals just long enough
to let new seals be born before they
go down to feed or be fed upon.
—Come sliding now, and later we'll
go swimming, dive in with the
muskrats, black bass, water moccasins, under
this willow let the prairie wind
drink from our bare skin:
good water
fits every mouth.

3

White Eagle, Early

Some years before we walked on that pond's ice, the first photograph of my twin sister and me was taken. Two babies, less than a year old, sit propped against an Indian blanket, looking solemnly into the camera. My baby-shirt's sleeves are grimy, and the Indian blanket is old and tired. The story our folks always told when we were looking at this picture—which I still have, passed on to me after my mother died in 1981—is that it was taken when Maxine and I were being taken care of by Uncle Woody, Aunt Jewell, and her Ponca folks in the Ponca tribal village, White Eagle—fifty miles to the west of Pawhuska, the Osage Agency town where we were born.

They kept us there through much of a year when our mother had split with our mixed-blood Osage father but was not yet married to our fullblood Osage stepfather. Uncle Woody (our mother's brother) was probably staying over at White Eagle to hide out from the law, which likely wanted him for bootlegging. He stayed over there so much he was learning to speak Ponca pretty well, they used to say. Aunt Jewell tells me that one day a photographer came by their house and said he was giving special prices for children. They told him it just happened that their twin niece and nephew were there for a little while and at those rates why not take a picture of them? So they set us up there, with no special preparations, just propped us against the blanket in the clothes we were wearing. The photographer set the camera up, and there we are.

Way later, when I was living in St. Louis, I used to drive down to Oklahoma two or three times a year to visit Osage and Ponca folks.

Uncle Woody and Aunt Jewell had left Oklahoma in 1946, when he got back from his World War Two time with the Seabees in the Aleutian Islands, and they headed out to Nevada, and then California and elsewhere, where there were lots of jobs and they worked at many of them over the next decade and more. They left with four kids and had two more while they were out there, and for a good many years lived in Porterville, north of Bakersfield and south of Stockton, in the Central Valley of California not far from Sequoia and Kings Canyon National Parks.

About 1970 though, my cousins came back, and a little later so did Aunt Jewell and Uncle Woody, who had split up. She remarried, and with the new husband moved back into Ponca tribal housing in White Eagle where she lived until 1999, having been joined there by some of the children and grandchildren in shifting groups and arrangements, though after a while cousin Craig and family set up house a few miles south and a little west in the hamlet of Marland (where about 1930 our Uncle Carter Camp had robbed the bank and got shot), and cousin Casey and her family lived in Fairfax (on the Osage Reservation) for a while and then moved over to Red Rock, some miles more south and west.

Uncle Woody, after working over in Enid as a security guard, and living in Pawhuska for a while, moved over to Ponca City, six miles north of White Eagle, and lived there from the 1980s till he died in 1995.

The first of the two White Eagle poems below, "Making a Name," looks at a time when I was maybe three years old and my twin sister and I were staying over with Aunt Jewell and folks for some time there. The second one, "Paint and Feathers," sets beside each other the "old ways" and the "now ways."

Making a Name

The authors of this story are
my Ponca folks, Aunt Jewell and
Uncle Woody. I'm directing the movie
made from the story.
So come on with us! Here we go now,

you hear them laughing everywhere as we
         are looking down from the sky,
        dodging a bewildered buzzard here to
    float over the asphalt licorice-strips of
this Interstate, I-44 it is—
      look out! we're heading for a cloud,
    the hail and wind are blinding us,
      we're in the cloud and whirling, now
    the cloud turns dazzling white before us and
    we break out into sunlight behind a brilliant
      white wall of cloud, above us
    the cobalt blue sky, below—
              aha!
   you see that red line there,
      the Oklahoma line! Aunt Jewell laughing,
we zoom southwest over the rain-drenched green as
      rectangles of winter wheat sparkle
    behind us in the sun-path leading
      eastward beneath a line of thunderstorms
    straight into the morning sun, but look
      ahead now, the silver shallow meanders of
the Arkansas, on this side here the Osage
      Reservation, on that Western side
the Ponca lands—
      now we can see
        Uncle Woody gunning
a Model A coupe down U.S. 77 heading
    to Anadarko maybe, he and Uncle Gus,
and we're coming down,
      we're circling on the wings
    of this red-tailed hawk above the
straggle of houses, clapboard with the white
      paint nearly gone,
      and there
    on the back porch of one old house a
small boy stands with his foot—
    what's that he's standing with his foot in

up to the knee almost—
a SLOP-bucket filled
with garbage for the pigs,
cold water with greasy scraps
of lettuce, tomatoes, greasy biscuits floating!
That little kid, whoo, LISten to him swear!
Listen, my God it's ME—
I still remember how that cold
water came up my leg,
see, I was going out
from this back door, here, into the yard this
morning, going to play in
those rain-puddles there, but stepping
off the back porch had my eyes entirely on
that great big Dominecker rooster watching
me stand here swearing now, and
watching him I stepped off with one foot into
this bucket here—
"But what I can't get over,"
Aunt Jewell tells us, laughing still,
still not grey-haired, no,
now her seventieth birthday coming up,
but here on the back porch
she's not yet twenty, just come out to see
what in the world her little nephew
is cussing so steadily about,
"—what I can't get over
is that you NEVER took your foot out, juuust stood there
cussing a blue streak at your foot and at
that big slop-bucket.
My, you could swear!
Here you were this little three-year-old—
I guess you picked up all those words
from your Grandpa Camp when he was plowing
the garden up that month and you had followed
with him behind the mules and plow,
and those were real *lazy* mules!

So when I came out there
on the porch to see you, Mike, to see
what you were swearing at, why there you stood,
with one foot in the slop-bucket, just
cussing a blue streak.
You know, my blind
great-aunt, she was in the back bedroom,
she heard you there, she was amazed.
"My goodness," she said. "Listen
to that boy, where'd he learn to talk like that?"
She was really old by then,
she'd come down to Oklahoma when us Poncas
were forced down from Nebraska
back in the 1870s.
Oh, we laughed and laughed
about it, all the time we took you in
and cleaned your leg and shoes up,
she told me, "You sure have got a smart nephew,
daughter, to know all those bad words."

—Well, of course I had good teachers,
I learned my English words from experts,
but who knows,
the chance to practice ALL of them
might never have come to me had I not lived
for some time in my youth with my feet
set firmly on an Indian Reservation.
Ah, here we are now, back
in St. Louis, *Gateway To The West*—
and how'd you like flying under the Arch
with real live Indians, this time?

4

White Eagle, Later

By the 1970s, when Aunt Jewell and our Ponca folks moved from
California back to White Eagle, there were brick Tribal Housing
homes there and she moved into one that came vacant. She and her
new husband Joe planted cedar trees, and apple trees, and a cotton-
wood tree from a piece she brought down from the Sun Dance,
around the place, and they grew with astonishing speed, and an
oriole—a Sun Bird, I call it—wove its hanging nest and raised its
young in that Sun Dance tree.

She and my cousins and the kids began going up, each
summer, to the Sun Dance on the Rosebud Reservation—the one
at Crow Dog's Paradise, since Leonard Crow Dog had been the
medicine man inside Wounded Knee during the occupation of it in
March and April 1973 by traditional Oglala people and American
Indian Movement members of whom Carter Camp was a national
leader. Her grandchildren were of an age to find the things grandchildren can get into trouble with, and one of the grandchildren was
drowned in a branch of Salt Creek down near the Ponca Powwow
grounds. Things were a long way from peaceful or easy at White
Eagle, and when I visited sometimes as I would drive with Aunt
Jewell along the streets or roads there, we would see some of the
young people walking in the way this poem tells.

Paint and Feathers

Into a star   Now put your face into
You have cast yourself,   this brown paper bag filled

have made your body of
the male star who touches
the sky with crimson
that I touch now upon
your face so you
may move upon the path
of life as does the young
sun at dawn surging
upward in scarlet and
traveling against all
who would stop him
across the sky to leave
it bright with rose and gold.
As he moves, as he first
rises, two plumes
fly upward from his head
at the horizon, white
eagle plumes I fasten now
into your hair, so you
may have the sun's power
and travel with him.
When he stands centering
the blue sky, every color
streams from him; here
I fasten round your neck
this disc of mussel shell,
mother of pearl, round sun,
so you may stand and see
all life within your vision,
all colors of it in
horizon's circle, changing
and still as sun at noon.
Here from the buffalo
this bit of fat I touch
upon your hair, what fills
your deepest hungers for
the life of this world now

with aluminum spray-paint,
breathe in, reel back,
shudder, stagger now.
Walk now along this asphalt,
stumble, your eyes wide
and blank, white paint across
your face, move towards
the old dance grounds,
and wave your arms to make
the car get over, go around
your slack blinded saunter.
The dead bird there crawling
with ants, the scissortail,
eyes eaten out, the rose
underwing color showing: take
it up, drop it, fumble, pull
tail-feathers loose and jam
them in your hair. The ants
crawl down across your eyes,
they stop and twiddle at
the paint. In the house,
where wires catch waves of
pictures from across the earth,
they ask for you. You climb
into the car, you drive northward
without headlights, straight
into the other car. Flashing
red patrol-cars come and find
the bodies mingled with metal
and plastic, white paint
spattered inside your car,
they do not notice feathers
from scissortails blowing in
the midnight wind. The far vision
inside the house tells of deaths
across the sea tonight, but in
the red and gray dawn as the first

will meet you on your way
as you are moving on the path
of sun and of the stars.
Now you are prepared
to take your name, here
in the House of Mystery
our words have made to be
the world in which we move
in which our people bear
the sun, the stars, their
bodies move to meet old age
and reach the happy days.

white plumes of sunlight shoot
up from the east, it will speak
of driving in the wrong
direction, children killed,
those who will not live
to see old age, those blinded
by metal paint and headlights
whiting out the stars.
At the Sun Dance, Little Brother,
we will dance for you, the feather
will fly, *xu-be,* up past the knot,
to where we hear you laughing.

5

Buck Creek to Oxford by Birch Canoe

Even with a voice, a song, and one kind of name, there was the matter of "placing" the voice—*locating a self*. Maybe a good piece to illustrate how this worked at times for me, in my mixed red-and-white heritage, is the piece using an Old English poetic form (the "riddle," a dramatic monologue in alliterative half-lines) to let an American Indian "space ship"—alias birchbark canoe—tell how it gets around this world. I picked up the riddle form when I was getting the B.A. in English at Oxford University, and years later when I used it to let a Birch Canoe tell its story, I came to understand that this was also my story: the bringing into being of a mixed self, afloat between cultures and times, between heaven and earth, between North America and Europe—another way of being "transported" into and through time.

Birch Canoe

Red men embraced   my body's whiteness,
cutting into me   carved it free,
sewed it tight   with sinews taken
from lightfoot deer   who leaped this stream—
now in my ghost-skin   they glide over clouds
at home in the fish's   fallen heaven.

"Birch Canoe" is a riddle poem, written in Old English alliterative meter and in the form of such riddles as those in the tenth-century Exeter Book. To compose a riddle, the scop or writer listens for how some ordinary thing might describe its extraordinary being. The riddle is what this creature tells us of itself, from which we are supposed to guess its name and nature. Old English riddles are spoken, for instance, by a hawk or a hunting-horn, a Bible or a bookworm, a swan or ship's anchor, an onion or a man's shirt, by a thunderstorm or by the Cross of Christ. In each of these the created being speaks through a wordsmith, telling how it came into being, what it does, sometimes how it interacts with human beings.

The extant Old English riddles mostly do not have titles—their readers are expected to figure out for themselves the "solution" to each poem, deducing from its internal clues who the speaker is.[1] If the answers were always obvious there would be no fun, and to have some fun, to be part of a social game, is one reason riddles were composed and recited or copied and read. In one of these mystery-poems, its telltale footprints might lead back to very different doors or dens, and sometimes they would lead through red-light districts, so to speak—although in most of these, the naughtiness turns out to be only in the listener's or reader's mind.

One mysterious creature, for instance, tells us with deadpan double entendre how a lady will pat and knead it until it rises—and then it turns out the creature speaking is bread dough! I should mention, however, that our modern word *lady* derives from the Old English word *hlæf-diga*, "loaf-kneader," and our word *lord* comes from *hlæf-weard*, "loaf-guardian," so an Anglo-Saxon listener or reader must have been very used to the double entendres in the Bread Dough riddle.

I hasten to point out that my twentieth-century Birch Canoe carries nothing the least bit naughty. The canoe tells how those who created it did so by cutting the white bark off a birch tree, carving it into canoe shape, and sewing it together. Of course I should have said they used tamarack roots for the sewing, but I figured *some* of the binding might have been with tendons or sinews, so I dragged those deer-ligaments in, just so as to link that featherlight canoe with those lightfoot deer. Getting the deer in gave the poem plot and narrative flow: the windfoot deer once leaped the stream where now the white birch canoe floats lightly with the men who made it.

And once the canoe got itself created and set on the stream, it could show us how it moves between heaven and earth, as if in a heaven of reflected clouds, and quite literally on the water, fallen from heaven, which now is the fish's home.

I hope the reader will see that these words create red men who take white bark and make it into a way of moving in this stream, whatever heaven or earth it may be; and that my being a mixed-blood Osage and white person is part of the double vision which the riddle allows. I have no idea whether some of the Old English riddlers inscribed "autobiographical" elements into their riddles, but I would not be surprised—if we ever recovered evidence on the biographies of the riddlers, including the dates and circumstances of their composing particular poems—to find that they did. It seems more likely, however, that what was inscribed had as much to do with the politics and social relations of the beer-hall or monastery as with the individual writer. Riddles were not "Romantic" projections of a writer's psyche so much as participation in the social dynamics of the writer's time and place.

I think, as a mere amateur reader of Old English poetry, that by the tenth century, when the largest extant gathering of Old English riddles was copied into the manuscript known as the Exeter Book, "pagan" Germanic riddles were being transubstantiated, as it were, from bread-loaves into Eucharist-wafers. One such genetically altered piece, I believe, is the "Swan" riddle, which I have translated into modern English. (The Exeter Book manuscript, into which this poem was copied, is still owned by Exeter Cathedral and I think is still viewable in a display case there.) I have translated the riddle in a way that makes it (or perhaps reveals it to be) a poem about the human soul's being fashioned more for heavenly than for earthly heroics, and the unspoken implication of such a reading is that the poem was composed by, and for, a religious community—who knows, perhaps those of Exeter Cathedral itself. But when I read it to an audience, I like to mention that the Exeter Book used to be left open for view at a page marked by circular beer-stains from a mug or tankard which had been set there. Possibly the monk, or whoever thus desecrated the book, was in one way or another made to pay for so doing.

The Swan's Song

Garbed in silence   I go on earth,
dwell among men   or move on the waters.
Yet far over halls   of heroes in time
my robes and the high   air may raise
and bear me up   in heaven's power
over all nations.   My ornaments then
are singing glories,   and I go in song
bright as a star,   unstaying above
the world's wide waters,   as a wayfaring soul.

6

Some Worldly Riddles
Trinity and Skunk

There are other ways of being transported; here are some more riddles spoken by creatures who can do it. The first one is a wilder creature with three natures who tells a little of what she does, and in the "Trinity" piece below inscribes bold-faced anagrams of her three names. Such clues to a riddle-being's name and nature were used by Old English poets like Cynewulf, who "signed" their poems not with boldface type, as here, but inserting here and there Germanic runes instead of Latin-alphabet characters—so that a reader who knew runes could put together those alien letters into anagrams of the speaking creature's name, or perhaps that of the poet.

The other archaic feature I have used in this first piece is calling it a "trinity" riddle. Old Christian exegetes were fond of pointing to "natural signs" thought to illuminate for human observers the great mystery of the Triune Nature of God. William Langland, in his long allegorical poem *Piers Plowman,* used the example of fingers closed into a fist. I don't put this riddle forward as Trinitarian, but I hope it catches the numinous flowing, floating, or shimmering near us.

A Trinity-Riddle

I spread, descending,   a samite of stars.
White fingers bring me   for breakfast Mont Blanc,
and I develop   on earth's negative

the prints proving   a presence absent.
Rainbow-dancing,   my restless soft-self
teaches the sun at   his summer turn to
reprise in dawn-prisms   the light-praise of plants,
or stars in winter   the still song-homes
with brittle jewels   dropped bright from darkness,
or shifts my shape to   a shimmering self-trap.
NOW Speak, if you spy it,   the sp**ECI**al name
I bear in spring when   I ba**RE TAW**dry alleys
to wear till dawn night-diamonds,   till dusk the jewel of time.

Riddles need not be all solemn and sacred. Here is a two-line epigram I made up to show students in a History of the English Language course how the alliterative meter worked. I needed a short, easily memorized example against which they could test lines they had composed to see if they were properly formed. Once when I was a boy, my Uncle Bert had shot a skunk that was killing our chickens, and my grandfather told us that in the good old days they used to eat the occasional skunk so killed. So at the cost of some very unpleasant skinning operations, and then some Colonel Sanders deep-frying time, we had a delicious meal, and found that fried skunk is less gamy than rabbit or squirrel, and tender as young chicken.

De Gustibus

To skin a skunk,   skill is needed—
but even fried   few will eat it.

The example worked—that is, the students turned out some pretty good short alliterative pieces.

7

Indian Survival, One

To return now to the small narrative of finding a voice, a song, a self, once they are found there is always the fight to keep them. Once we can word ourselves in a world, we have to find how to stay alive in song. One story about this I have called "Dancing with Dinosaurs." I was delighted when paleontologists noticed that dinosaurs have not died out, that what we hear singing at the windowsill is a tiny tyrannosaurus, as the earthworms have always known, trembling at the thunderous tread of a robin bobbing across the lawn to gobble them down.

I had loved to hear the birds begin their prayers, of a summer's morning in the Buck Creek Valley, as naturally as Milton's Adam and Eve sang Matin-Psalms in Eden. I always was mystified by their migrations, and I wondered what they had in mind as they darted up into the air of Louisiana and set sail for Yucatan. What maps do they use, what ancestral voices do they hear prophesying spring where they are headed?

Then I read in *National Geographic* and *Scientific American* of how the tiny black-and-white warblers in Nova Scotia and Maine take off in September and fly for three days and nights, Good Friday to Easter Sunday as it were, at the cold height of twenty thousand feet or more, over the whole Atlantic Ocean down to South America. I was not surprised, but I was and am amazed.

So when news came that even archaeologists now admitted what any careful observer of a back yard had always known, that these were small dinosaurs who had put on feathers and survived,

I suddenly understood better why we as Indian people put on our feathers to survive. I wished once again that the anthropologists who keep digging in the earth for our bones would listen for our songs in the air. We are extinct as dinosaurs, we are alive as birds, *who made their rainbow bodies long before we came to earth, who learning song and flight became beings for whom the infinite sky and trackless ocean are a path to spring.*

And because I was just then learning to be a Gourd Dancer, I wrote of our dancing in St. Louis as we brought into the circle of named beings the Comanche granddaughter of Bob and Evelyne Wahkinney Voelker, and how, as the gourds shook and their feathers fluttered, we knew that now she could cross with us. Here now is the poem itself:

Dancing with Dinosaurs

I.

Before we came to earth,
before the birds had come,
they were dinosaurs, their feathers
were a bright idea
that came this way:
see, two tiny creatures weighing
two ounces each keep quiet and among
the ferns observe bright-eyed
the monsters tear each other
and disappear; these two watch from
the edge of what, some fifty billion spins
of the cooling earth ahead, will be
called Nova Scotia—now, with reptilian
whistles they look southward as
Pan-Gaea breaks apart and lets
a young Atlantic send its thunder crashing
up to the pines where they cling
with minuscule bodies in a tossing wind,
September night in the chilly rain and
they sing, they spread

small wings to flutter out above
surf-spray and rise to
            twenty thousand feet on swirling
                winds of a passing cold front that lift
        them over the grin of sharks southeastward into sun
and all day winging under him pass high above
                the pink and snowy beaches of Bermuda flying
through zero cold and brilliance into darkness
                    then into moonlight over steel
    Leviathans with their mimic pines that call them down
            to rest and die—
                they bear
            southeast steadily but the Trade
                Winds come and float them curving
        back southward over the Windward Islands and
                southwestward into marine and scarlet of
            their third day coming down
                to four thousand feet still winging over
            Tobago, descending till
    the scaly waves stretch and feather into the surf of
                        Venezuela and they drop
            through moonlight down to perch
    on South America's shoulder, having become
            the Male and Female Singers, having
        put on their feathers and survived.

2.

When I was named
            a Thunder person, I was told:
        here is a being
                of whom you may make your body
    that you may live to see old age: now
            as we face the drum
    and dance shaking the gourds, this gourd
                is like a rainbow of feathers, lightly
            fastened with buckskin,
        fluttering as the gourd is shaken.

The eagle feathers I
> have still not earned, it is
the small birds only
whose life continues on the gourd,
> whose life continues in our dance,
that flutter as the gourd is rattled and
> we dance to honor on a sunbright day
> and in the moonbright night
the little girl being brought in,
> becoming one of us,
> as once was done for me,
for each of us who dance.
> The small birds only, who have given
their bodies that a small girl
> may live to see old age.
I have called them here
> *to set them into song*
who made their rainbow bodies long before
> *we came to earth,*
who learning song and flight became
> *beings for whom the infinite sky*
> *and trackless ocean are*
a path to spring:
> *now they will sing and we*
> *are dancing with them, here.*

8

Getting Across
Buck Creek to Skye and Back

In the ordinary world, I can remember a time when there were birds all around us while some of us dangled under a bridge—the kind of silly thing boys get up to for no reason other than daring each other—so that the birds and other creatures we barely noticed, as we hung between life and death, in memory are more intensely there, a part of our effort to survive. The swallows no doubt were alarmed that we were close to their nests, and for the sake of their children were no less glad than we that we made it across alive.

In spring 1972 I wrote a poem called "Getting Across" about that one time, thirty years earlier. It was one of the first poems I wrote that was not in blank verse or other "squared-off" line format, but in the "broken lines" which I have favored since October 1971. It appeared as one among a group that for a while I called "Skye Poems," because this change of style followed from a change in my way of seeing the world that took place when I went up to visit some former students on the Isle of Skye—an island of the Inner Hebrides, off the northwest coast of Scotland—where my friends Maude and Joe and Frankie lived while Maude was working on a doctorate in anthropology.

That was during a 1971–72 sabbatical I took which was meant for medieval research but went in considerable part, as it turned out, to writing poems. In June 1971 I had gone over to Oxford for work in the Bodleian Library there, but that was Nam and Hippie time, when even the Bodleian Library was having a hard time keeping scholarly articles from being stolen or slashed, and a lot of what I needed to look at was not so easy to get hold of, so I moseyed on up to the Isle of Skye and stayed for a while with my friends in the croft house at Skinidin, not far from Dunvegan Castle.

The peninsula was then and I hope still is a Gaelic-speaking area, where Maud could study Gaelic naming and inheritance patterns, Frankie could paint, and Joe could write and help make life good with guitar and chess and a way he had of opening the natural and trans-natural to each other. For some weeks in the late summer and early autumn, we hiked all over the Dunvegan Peninsula, and looking down one day from McLeod's Table, the highest point on that peninsula, watching the streams go flashing silvery down glen and dale and waterfall to the ocean, and seeing the peninsula hold like a gentle hand its fields and houses, I wanted my hand to hold the Buck Creek Valley that way.

So walking on Skye made me change style, from squared blank-verse story and dramatic monologue to verse that cascaded down like a mountain stream on Skye but made fresh channels for Mnemosyne, Mother of the Muses, in Oklahoma. An early poem I wrote in this new way was begun in October 1971:

> *Walking with Friends Down Lorigill and Dibadal,*
> *on the Isle of Skye*
>
> Coming down from the watershed's pools
> we drank first at the source
> of Lorigill, sliding silent
> from under its green turf, dark
> and swift—
> downstream we
> paused
> where strawcolored riffles twittered,
> saw the turquoise quiver
> of ocean brimming its notch
> of gunsight vale, opening gradually
> as we walked down into

a wineglass slowly drained
    of the sea's blue flashes from its crystal
  of air and green dale—
    then the streamwater deepened
to a Chablis cataract shooting
    its long roils of bubbles down into chasms
of burgundy water alive with
    marblings of white foam slowly
  swirling on blackness into quick
wild-geese-flights of bubbles down
    to the next rapids—
and down, down until the dale
    flattened, where its stream
went swaying amber over pebbles
      among ruined stone walls
  greened over with turf, enclosing
    tall foxgloves strung with orbwebs—
    and slid through abandoned fields
  ribbed with green furrows under
bracken staggering up toward enormous
boulders fallen from scarp-heights and wearing
    green-vivid mosses; and we
stretched a crystal moment under
    bracken's brown
      jungle-palms over
  neat English lawn
      dew-sparkling,
we saw the pebble-boulder in that glen with its
    black slug-monster feeding
    in pale gold light—
then we rose and waded through bracken down
    the gradual slope to pebbles where
the sliding stream
  moved into surf,
      its gentle light into
  sandfilled thunder—
    we walked there over

dry roundings at ebbtide of soft
brown eggs among pink discs and black slate-bowls
askew on mottled
greybrown loaves until there came
a sudden dark splash on one from
a raindrop falling
down from a steam-gray cloud in
its cornflower sky—then
a spitting of sleetballs bouncing
dryly off rocks while the raindrops splashed loose
red flames in the
brown rocks or ripped
blue streaks down gray ones and polished
whole pebbles to agate—
and when the icy shower pulled back up the dale
it twinkled over green
high slopes where the sun broke
through in a rainbow
drifting across green ploughland
frosted with rain—
and we climbed up from the beach
behind the dwindling shower
to the shepherds' hut and
sprawled out for lunch
above the stream's rippling,
being careful not to break the ruby
and glabrous lemon mushrooms spilled
by the rainbow's passing over
green springy turf
back into the heart
of sunlight and falling rain.

Once I got back to the United States and drove down to visit
my folks in the Buck Creek Valley, I remembered, as I drove across
the U.S. 60 bridge over Buck Creek, the dangerous crossing we
made, Walter and Toby and my brother Antwine and I. They had
inveigled me into swinging across the creek on the girders below the

bridge, and I paused midway in fright, while the little barn-swallows with their nests under there were darting past and around and below me there. Remembering, in spring 1972 I wrote "Getting Across," which some years later helped jump-start a lecture to the new members of Phi Beta Kappa at the University of Tulsa in May 1990.

Forty years before the lecture, I had suffered through speeches by people who had been students forty years before that. It seemed that people from the last decade of the nineteenth century were *getting across,* through me, to those new Phi Betes in the last decade of the twentieth century. The simple fact was that most of the listeners had known their grandparents, who knew *their* grandparents—so most could truthfully claim their direct memory spanned at least five generations, and since they in turn would be speaking to grandchildren yet unborn, it would make seven generations directly in touch with each other—two hundred years or so of *getting across* time in fairly direct fashion.

But speaking to them, I thought: how far from each other, how often out of touch, are parents and children—how little the children know of what their grandparents actually think and feel and how they came to be that way, how small the number of stories that remain about great-great-grandparents in our culture, where nothing is remembered unless it is written or taped. How hard it is, to *get across* the distances of family history—let alone national or international history!

For that matter, it's a long way from one person to another— a red phone or hotline isn't enough to get us over that distance. *Some* things do cross by regular routes—the InterState bridges of solid prose where carloads of good sense roar through. Myself, I like thinking back to that time when I was trying to swing across, hand over hand, *beneath* the bridge—where possibility seesawed with reality, where life was fragile, dumb, unauthorized. Fifty years before my lecture-moment, I had stood watching as the WPA rebuilt that Buck Creek bridge, had heard the dynamite blast out rock for its concrete foundations, had seen the chunks of old concrete with their rusting steel rods sticking up in the deep water below the bridge—and later, dangling below the bridge, I saw how far it was from the east bank to the west, how far I would fall if I didn't make it over, which rod might impale me if I dropped just right, what depth might drown or rock might shatter me if I fell elsewhere.

That's one way I got across Buck Creek, before I had thought or even knew about a university, let alone a Phi Beta Kappa Society. The education I got in passing was not from any of my regular teachers, and others who graduated there will have followed a different syllabus or curriculum, but here is my transcript from that U.S. 60 bridge over Buck Creek:

Getting Across

Hanging
           out under the bridge
     by fingertips and a toe
                    between ledge and girder, high
       over deep water and thinking,
               I can't swim,
       unreachable by the older boys
                    who've made it across, he watches
          the steelblue flashing of wings
     and chestnut bellies of barnswallows
                 shooting and swirling around him,
                          below him,
       a two-foot gar's black shadow
                    in the greenbrown water, and before
     he has weakened lets
                          the toe slip gently and swings
               down like a pendulum, hand over
          hand along the girder to where
                          the others perch
                                 on the concrete ledge,
          has kicked up his right leg onto
                    the ledge and is
          pulled to its safety, can look back
                    now at the swallow's easy
          curve upwards, its

flutter and settling

gently into the cup

of feather-lined mud there nestling

on the shining girder's side

where he has passed his death.

A new-fledged swallow hesitates before it drops from its nest, and there is considerable twittering. The body must seem impossibly heavy, like a human's coming out of the sea onto rocks, and surely it feels dangerous to tip over the edge, but something makes it irresistible. Gravity calls, and once she befriends them, they fall, wings of lightness and joy take over, they skim between banks, down to the stream where nestmates are dipping and drinking, they pass each other upwards, downwards, at home in air—they get across. A gift of feathers makes the air their home, the wind their friend, Gravity their godmother.

Up on the roadway, though, it was another story. I noticed dead swallows now and then along the highway, where they had maybe lost an argument with a truck, though swallows may sometimes just drop from the air when they are ready to die, so a jury might have found the accused Mack or Peterbilt as innocent as Frankenstein. Very different beings, each pursuing life and liberty and happiness, those Juggernauts and the little New Age dinosaur-birds who'd long ago put on feathers and survived the asteroids, and who may yet survive our invention of the Wheel, and Engines, and Asphalt Roads with Ditches that define our goals and direct our movements at deadly cross-purpose to theirs.

But what of the insects those swallows hunt, glittering in the air or smashing against our windshields? *They* took to the air before the dinosaurs did; they found themselves a freedom and speed no earthbound creatures could match, crossed from Here to There as they pleased. And THEN the dinosaurs took wing, new quick feathers let them hunt down those gnats and mosquitoes, those mating ants and lacewings: Swifts and Swallows rode the wind and did to ancient insects what trucks do now to swallows—though birds did it to eat, not just at random.

Yet if insects had out-of-body visions, they'd be laughing to see along every road seething masses of earthbound ants and maggots, feasting on birds brought down by the rumbling monsters of our prime time, manna dropped by monstrous human gods roaring past. What goes around, comes around—birds feast on flying ants, crawling ants feast on birds, humans just keep on trucking. And except for the roadkill, all these trucks and swallows leave no trace—roads and bridges keep no tracks. For human beings a bridge is safe on top, dangerous beneath, but for swallows it's the other way round.

Well, the road is mostly safe and entertaining for us, but it does dictate where we can go, and cars tell us how we must get there—but not all they say is gospel. When I try to get BACK across, a different kind of country music is needed to cross that bridge.

Driving in Oklahoma

On humming rubber along this white concrete,
lighthearted between the gravities
of source and destination like a man
halfway to the moon
in this bubble of tuneless whistling
at seventy miles an hour from the windvents,
over prairie swells rising
and falling, over the quick offramp
that drops to its underpass and the truck
thundering beneath as I cross
with the country music twanging out my windows,
I'm grooving down this highway feeling
technology is freedom's other name when
—a meadowlark
comes sailing across my windshield
with breast shining yellow
and five notes pierce
the windroar like a flash
of nectar on mind,
gone as the country music swells up and drops
me wheeling down
my notch of cement-bottomed sky

between home and away
and wanting
to move again through country that a bird
has defined wholly with song,
and maybe next time see how
he flies so easy, when he sings.

When I think of traveling between past and future, bringing things I value with me, there's a poem by the Acoma Pueblo poet Simon Ortiz that I think of. He wrote it as the seventh of his "Forming Child" poems (it is among the poems in his great collection *Woven Stone,* published by the University of Arizona in 1992), at a time when one of his children was forming in the mother's womb:

Forming Child Poems
Seven

Near the summit, SE of Kinlichee,
I saw a piece of snowmelt water
that I thought would maybe look good
on a silver bracelet with maybe
two small turquoise stones at its sides;
but then, I liked the way it was, too,
under pine trees, the snow feeding it,
the evening sunlight slanting off it,
and I knew that you would understand
why I decided to leave it like that.

This has not yet been canonized as one of the great poems of our age, but it will be—though for Simon's sake I hope not for many years, since it is much harder to write great poems when people are telling you what a great poet you are, and wanting you to write more poems just like those that once were given to you. We like what we know, and we want the same when it comes to our favorite poems and songs: play it again, Simon! But what he has done here is to keep that memory of a particular place and time, that track of his past, and hand it over to the child. He has "left it like that," and yet he has also taken it as gift to the child yet unborn. He has given it to anyone who can read or hear English and shares the gift of human sight and feelings. It is a turquoise and silver bracelet put into words, but as with the real silver and turquoise work of Pueblo people, it is also the mountain, snow-water, pine trees, the natural world who are invited to come and live in the work of silversmith or wordsmith who can craft a story with a little world inside it like good medicine, getting across its human and natural and divine gift of meaning.

Osage and Ponca Family Members

My mother, Thelma Camp, had seven children, the eldest being Antwine Pryor (b. 1929), the next two being Maxine and me (b. 1931). In 1933 she married Addison Jump, son of Jacob and Josephine Jump, and elder brother of Arita, Louis, and Kenneth Jump. Addison and Thelma had four half-Osage children: Ireta ("Josie," b. 1934), Louis James ("Jim," b. 1936), Josephine Marie ("Sister," b. 1938), and Addison Jr. ("Junior," b. 1941).

Jacob Jump (Osage grandfather), c. 1910–15.

Jacob and Josephine Jump and their sons, Addison and Louis, c. 1917–18.

Arita Jump (aunt), c. 1932–33.

Addison and Thelma Jump and their daughter Ireta, c. 1934–35.

Students at the Chilocco Indian School, 1948. Ireta ("Josie") Jump is in the front row, fifth from right.

Louis James Jump ("Jim,") on his way to Korea, 1955.

Aunt Jewell McDonald at age fifteen, c. 1929.

In 1934, Thelma's brother Woodrow Camp married Jewell McDonald. They had six half-Ponca children: Darlena (1935), Dwain ("Bucky," 1937), Carter Augustus (1941), Cordell (1943), Craig (1946), and Katherine ("Casey," 1948).

A McDonald family portrait at White Eagle, Oklahoma, c. 1904–5. Charles McDonald— the father of Augustus ("Uncle Gus," b. 1898), Johnny, Jewell (b. 1914), and other children—is the man in the black hat at center back, holding Johnny. Gus is in the second row, third from left (with cap). Second row from top, in profile, is Louisa McDonald, the blind great-aunt who made the "strong-heart" song for Poncas after they were forced to walk from Nebraska to Oklahoma, a walk all the older people in this photograph must have made. (Photo by The Glass Negative, Ponca City, Oklahoma)

My Ponca relatives and I at the St. Louis Powwow, Jefferson Barracks Park, St. Louis, September 1990. Aunt Jewell is seated front and center, and her daughter Casey is at her left, with Bucky behind Casey. At back, left to right, are Carter Camp and his wife Linda. Their sons Ahn-bus-ska and Gus are in front of them. I am next (in cap) and then two other grandchildren of Aunt Jewell: Suzeta (daughter of Casey) and Amelia (daughter of Darlena).

Cousins Dwain ("Bucky") and Craig Camp, holding the Eagle Staff made for and given to them by Bob and Evelyne Wahkinney Voelker (Comanche) at the first Washington University, St. Louis, American Indian Powwow in March 1991.

9

Back Over to Doe Creek

Sometimes, in Oklahoma, when my younger brothers and sisters had got old enough, we would walk up through the meadow and stoop between the strands of the barbed-wire fence on its northwest side, and on up the round hill to its west that we called "Bockius's Hill." That was the last fence for a long time, where the real woods began—the dense blackjack-oak forest of the Osage Hills on the west and north sides of our valley, where Buck Creek came down from western prairie and Doe Creek came down from northern prairie, meeting in a tangle of rich bottomland where Buck Creek turned south toward the highway—but we usually went only over the hill and back toward where Doe Creek came down from the north to join Buck Creek.

Once, when my younger sisters Ireta and Josephine and brother Jim were old enough to walk with me, on a bright Saturday morning we headed out, down past our pond, through the barbed-wire fence and on up that Hill and into its woods. We took fishing poles and worms for when we'd got over its ridge and down again to Buck Creek, but we mostly wanted, like the Bear Who Went Over The Mountain, to see what we could see—and maybe it was only the Other Side Of The Mountain, but it seemed a different kind of place. Its creatures, animal and other, were watching us and they were telling us things. I put some of this into "Behind the Hill," which came out in the *Massachusetts Review* in 1960 and is in *Cowboys and Indians, Christmas Shopping:*

Behind the Hill

I remember that afternoon when we first came to the place
Where Doe Creek runs into Buck Creek. We climbed Bockius's Hill
That loomed on our west horizon like a huge green sun furred
    over with trees—
Up from the meadows and past where the gypsies camped,
    on into the woods
At last to its blackjack-and-bouldered top. A bluejay's feather
    moved, on a grey
Rock worn hollow by waters, grown soft with lichens.
    We heard no sound,
And nothing else moved, on the level hill's top among
    the straight trunks,
But we felt the animals hiding, the breath of wind, standing there
Quiet and scared till a crow's caw, down by the creek
The other side of the hill, told us the black birds
Were drifting, high in granite boughs of redoaks
    along the creekbanks,
Drifting and wondering where the noisy children with
    long poles had gone.
And when we went leaping down the hillside with buckets of worms
We stopped at a bee-tree the Bockius kids had felled last August,
Picked out crumbs of sugary wax, tasted their smoke
    and soft punkwood.
Down by the hill's foot, the hickory nuts were small and green,
But the squirrels already trying them: we scared a big grey squirrel
Out of his hickory and watched his fluid grappling dash
Over supple treetops to a solid oak. We left our dog barking
And followed a cow-trail through high green brush
    down toward the creek.
The path was bare, black, soft; a coon's fresh tracks were in it,
Wedge-heeled hind foot, spatulate-fingered front, five minutes old.
We came out by the deep hole at the creek-bend, walked out on a rock
To look down, were scared by a shitepoke's cry and rush of flight
From the opposite shore. It winged upstream, around the next bend.
"Let's go on after it," Jim said, "We can slip up on him maybe."

So we went, stepping quietly in soft grass,
    stooping through undergrowth,
And farther than we had ever gone, hunting the flown bird,
Till we came to a glade, on a little point of land,
With a shallow stream in front we'd never seen
    flowing into Buck Creek,
So quiet a cardinal seemed loud, whistling from over the stream.
We waded down the clear stream's soft-sanded bottom to Buck Creek
Where a rippled sand-bar went shelving down
    into blue-black depths
And a light current was tumbling sandgrains down from its edge
Past little sunperch at play there, finning themselves and yawning,
Drifting down in the undertow, riding an upsurge,
Rainbow stains on their backs and sides; or darting up
To strike at the little green worms who dripped from their elms
On the still surface. It was good fishing, but they
    came so easy to our hooks
They jostled in darting crowds till one was yanked fighting aloft
And flipped on the sandy banks; and they were too small to keep,
We threw them back and watched them vanish into blue-dark depths.
They always came back to play, but not quite so casually,
And in deeper water. After a while we gave up fishing,
We sprawled on the fine heavy sand under shifting elm-shadows
And water-sparkle. Down in the deep hole, a monstrous bass
Lunged at a dragonfly and missed with a vicious splash.
Then "Look!" Jim said. Sister and I turned our heads and saw
Slithering and floating down Doe Creek a water-moccasin.
Soundless and gleaming dark in the sunlit water
    he was carried near us,
Head up and eyes glittering so near we saw elliptic
    cat-pupils contracted
To slits, his shadow on the sand beneath him. Sliding
    past the sand-bar's edge
Out over the dark still pool he disappeared, but a moment later
Crawled out on a rock, on the other side, and lay there
    quiet in the sun.

10

Buck Creek
Walking North

We did a lot of walking, the years when I was maybe eleven to thirteen. To the north, if we wanted to walk barefooted up to visit friends in those hills, among the blackjack woods of the northern rim where the tornado had passed, we'd watch out a little more at first for anthills, rattlesnakes, and cow-pies, stepping through our hay-meadow to start the two-mile trek. And however spiky the bluestem hay, however the little thorns of its prairie roses might scrape our insteps, it was cooler for our feet walking through grass than on the dirt-and-gravel road that led from our meadow's north end up a steep hill that reached out toward us from the northern rim. On a really hot day when dust would bake and gravel bruise our bare feet, we'd have to wear shoes.

That county-graded road went curving steeply up round the hill's rocky cape—but we had to decide, at the hill's foot, whether to turn off to the right and visit the James kids, or keep going uphill to the Parkses. If we did turn right, we would climb down into and up out of the ditch that had eroded alongside the main road, and between strands of the nailed-and-wired-shut gate across to what used to be the road leading to the house below the James family's house. Maintaining a way for cars to cross that ditch, which carried off rainwater from down the steep hill, was always a struggle, and the families had finally given up and closed this southern road in— they now used only the fully graded and graveled northern lane.

So this southern way had grown over with grass and weeds, and to climb through the wired-up gate was a transgression. A kind of thrill went through us there, as if we were slipping in to sneak along beside the Osage-orange trees and past the wild plums and thick patches of blackberries in tall bluestem, under the persimmon trees in the grove that had grown up where the road swung behind a spur of the hill.

And hanging on that first gate sometimes, as we'd slip through, would be a carcass, a coyote once, another time a red-shouldered hawk, shot by a local rancher or teenage kid in the name of their chickens and pigs and calves, or just for the thrill of it. The coyote's subtle colors surprised me, but what dumbfounded me were the colors and hues, the patterns and rich variety of them, in the red-shouldered hawk's body. And my lord, those talons! the long curving terribly sharp thumb-claw and the lesser polished hooks of the others—and that hooked scary beak slightly open, those eyes eaten out by ants as the carcass dried and its stink faded. Beautiful, beautiful, all the streaks and bars of dark browns, buffs, orange mottling, the spread tail's stiff warm feathers fanned out there so precisely overlapping, the stretched wings nailed to keep their spread.

So often in the time before then, say when a pair of hawks circled over us in our yard while our chickens in the nearby fenced pen ran and cried and panicked, I had wanted to see the hawks closer, but even that once when a hawk—this time a redtail, I think—came down and briefly grabbed a Rhode Island Red hen before our dog Tip ran barking ahead of us to drive the hawk back into the air, even then I did not manage to see it close as I wanted. Nor could I ever manage to get close to a marsh hawk coursing over our meadow, not even when I saw one pounce, down by our pond, on a mouse, and I crouched, sneaked and circled, and tried to get close. And always those hawks on fenceposts or electric lines or in trees would take heavily to the air before I could get up and look at them. Binoculars were for rich educated people, in the big houses with rugs and easy chairs and sofas whose springs were not coming out, and that was before I had seen a bird-book, before the ninth- and tenth-grade science classes asked us to list our bird-sightings and gave us pictures to help. So that red-shouldered hawk was something I had been looking for, it seemed, a long time, nailed with spread wings on its gate where we could leave the traveled road and go along one grown with grass and flowers into a part of the country no longer used by the people around us, a place that felt like it was back to its own again.

Past the gate, the old overgrown road still had some of the smelter-cinders that had been spread on it when the Klepper family once lived on around the hill's bulge, in a house set at the ridge's foot, where blackjack and hickory trees hid the steep rise to the Big Rocks. When we turned off this way it was almost as much for the Big Rocks as it was to play with the James kids, Pat and Jimmie. Pat was in the same grade as my twin sister and me at Buck Creek, the one-room school a mile east in the valley, and Jimmy a couple of grades younger than her, so we had known them six years or so. Their dad did something in an office for Phillips Petroleum in Bartlesville, five miles east of us, but he liked the country and for several years they had rented an eighty-acre place from Jack Bockius down in the bluestem-prairie eastern end of the Buck Creek Valley, where Mr. James could run some cows and horses of his own, and now they had saved up enough to buy a house back in the woods on the valley's northern rim, with their back yard only a few hundred yards from the Big Rocks, and a view out over the whole green valley to the south and on to the wooded hills rising beyond. At night, from our place down on the meadow floor, we could see their light, dim and almost twinkling up there, if we stood on the right spot so the trees around their house didn't block it out. Which meant, I realized one day when we had actually gone on from the Big Rocks and Mrs. James gave us a piece of cake and some milk in their small white house, that they could see our house from their back yard.

I keep talking about these Big Rocks. They were great sandstone boulders that had fallen down the hillside and lay like beached whales and mini-mesas among the hickories and blackjacks and postoaks there. The smaller ones would be huge slabs, maybe three feet at the lower side, rising to six, eight, ten feet at the top, and it was fun to leap up on one of these and catfoot up to its high end and raise our arms in triumph like mountain-climbers. As we went

higher up the hill, toward the rimrock from which all these had broken loose and slid gradually down, the rocks seemed to get bigger,
and just below the edge the great rocks were splitting off from the
rim and there were crevasses and mini-canyons with the brown dead
leaves of many years mulching their floors, centipedes and snakes
crawling or coiling back in these shadowy cool places. We liked
climbing on some of these, dangerous enough for kids—maybe
thirty feet of sheer rock faces with knobs and eroded handholds,
sometimes the rockface slanting back so you were climbing up
around bulges and had to cling and sidle and reach a long way for a
hold. Once I got stuck and was afraid to go up or down and could
not go sideways and thought I was going to fall and die on the more
jaggedy rocks below, but just barely scuffed up and over the edge. It
leaves a tingle, a shocked slightly weakened exhilaration, to get away
with a climb like that, though if I looked at that boulder today it
would seem small enough and the drop was likely survivable, with a
little breakage and bruising.

The deepest "canyon" was near the very top, and if you
spreadeagled up one side of its smooth face you reached a little
mossy ledge and could look across the crevice to an even higher
ledge on the other side. There was what seemed to be a hawk's nest
there, but there was no way to get up to it on that side, and even if
we climbed on up this side the only way up led us around and
behind the great rock and we never got to look into the nest, if it
was a nest. Nor was it possible to get at the nest from the top of
that other side, which was the rim of the hill itself. The hawk or
whatever had placed it well. It was not more than three or four
hundred yards, I think, from the James house, and their kids came
down here to climb and poke around all the time, but the nest was
never bothered so far as I know. We did see the redtails circling a lot
over that part of the wooded hill, so it was probably theirs, and their
Seeeeirr! no doubt an official excommunication of trespassers on
hawk territory. Years later I would read the transcriptions of Osage
ceremonies made by the Omaha scholar Francis La Flesche for the
Smithsonian Institution's Bureau of American Ethnography, and
would see the description of the Hawk Shrine (or Medicine
Bundle), and I would think of the shivery feeling that hawk's nest

up there in the Big Rocks gave me when I looked up toward it, and I would say to myself the Osage word for the Hawk Shrine, *wah-ho-peh*. The shrine is in the Smithsonian now, I believe, and the ceremony in which it was essential is not presently used. Some of the names in our Thunder Clan are hawk names; my sister Ireta, who used to be along on our hikes up to those Big Rocks, carries one of these names.

But if we did not turn eastward toward those Big Rocks, and kept on walking north instead, up the curving steep hill and on to a T-junction—where we could turn west toward Bowring or east toward Butler Creek School and Bartlesville—we would turn west and go visit the Parks family, at least we did during that one endless year of 1941–42 when they lived in the small unpainted house in the blackjacks there, a mile and a half north of us. Their dad had been hired to manage some of the oil-well pumping machinery in that area, going around and checking the pumphouse engines and gear, greasing and fueling the well-pumps and rod-lines, turning them off or on to adjust the flow of oil, keeping tabs on the oil and gas stored in tanks, maybe collecting for his 1936 Ford V-8 a little of the low-octane "drip gas" that was a by-product of the wells.

Their son Walter was almost my age—his birthday was in March, nine days earlier than my own—and from his first days in Buck Creek School that fall of 1941 he and I were best buddies and were often at each other's house, if not out and away with dogs and a rifle on expeditions into the wooded hills, down along Doe Creek, Buck Creek, Sand Creek. Even after they moved miles eastward the next year, to the other side of Bartlesville, Walter and I would hitchhike back and forth to spend weekends. And when they moved back west again, away out west of Pawhuska to the prairie hamlet of Webb City stranded there among wheatfields and pastures like a starfish skeleton when the oil-boom tide had ebbed, we still exchanged weekend and summertime visits up into our high-school days. The summer we were eighteen, Walter and I went up to the Kansas wheat harvest and stayed on through August, working at plowing and house moving and construction that summer of 1949, earning money toward schooling that fall. A poem about that harvest work is printed in *Cowboys and Indians, Christmas Shopping,*

where I called it "In Kansas," but I have re-titled it now as
"Bringing in the Sheaves" so its implications might (I hope) be a
little clearer:

Bringing in the Sheaves

The '49 dawn set me high on a roaring yellow tractor,
slipping the clutch or gunning a twenty-foot combine
to spurt that red-gold wheat into Ceres's mechanical womb.
I'd set her on course and roll for a straight two miles
before turning left, and it got monotonous as hell—
at first all the roar and dust and the jiggling stems collapsing
to whisk up that scything platform and be stripped of their seed,
then even the boiling from under of rats and rabbits scrambling
to hide again in their shrinking island of tawny grain
as the hawks hung waiting their harvest of torn fur and blood.
So I'd play little god with sunflowers drooping their yellow heads—
would see a clump coming, and spin the wheel right,
     left, right, straight,
so the shuddering combine swiveled on its balljoint hitch
first right, then left, that great chatter of blades would go swinging
so the tip barely brushed those flowers and left their
     clump standing
like a small green nipple out from the golden breastline,
     and next time past
reversing wheel-spins cut free a sinuous lozenge left
     for the bumblebees,
its butter-and-black-velvet tops limp-nodding over wilted leaves.
But sunflowers weren't enough, I left on the slick stubble islets
of blue-flowered chicory, scarlet poppies, and just for
     the hell of it, cockleburrs:
"From now on, kid, you run that sumbitch straight!" the farmer said.
You know, out on that high prairie I bet the goldfinches,
bobwhites and pheasants *still* are feasting in that farmer's fields
from the flower-seeds I left out, summer, fall and winter harvests
that make the bread I eat taste better by not
              being ground up with it, then or now.

After that summer, I hardly got to see Walter or his folks for many years. In 1950, the year Korea became a place where our brothers and friends were taken to kill or be killed, he went into the army—surviving the Inchon landings where they slogged ashore in pounding surf under heavy fire—and my road took me then to Oxford and Yale and later St. Louis, his to other parts of Oklahoma, and we lost track of each other for a long time, though my mother would always tell me, when I'd get home to Buck Creek now and then, of where the Parkses were living at the time, some in Oklahoma City, some out toward the Panhandle. Finally in 1989, when I had a visiting professorship at the University of Oklahoma, I was able to drive up and visit with Walter and his wife and kids in Kingfisher and hear how all his folks were doing while we ate the huge lunch they'd fixed, and in 1994 Walter and his wife Carol, and his sister Mary Ellen and her husband Calvin Parker (in whose house we roomed during that 1949 wheat harvest, on the Kansas prairie near the hamlet of Palco), came up to Ponca City where I was giving a poetry reading, and we had a good time talking there, along with my Ponca folks—Aunt Jewell and family—and my Uncle Woody.[2]

That was more than fifty years after the Parkses had moved into our Buck Creek neighborhood from Rock Creek, in the wooded hills and canyons to the west of us toward Sunset Lake. Mrs. Parks was part Cherokee, daughter of a man who had been a U.S. marshal before statehood; Mr. Parks was a huge quiet man, six feet four and maybe two hundred thirty pounds, not obviously muscular but both powerful and astonishingly nimble when necessary—he could stand on the edge of a swimming pool and turn a front flip into the water. He had a ready smile and no great opinion of himself, but even though he never acted tough, hardly spoke, and was always courteous, people walked and talked with courtesy around him. In that time and place a big strong nice-looking man like him might have had a honkytonking urge now and then, but if Mr. Parks did I never heard of it. Even in the roughest of beer-joints he could have been a bouncer, able to take any potential troublemaker out the door, no need to get rough maybe. His wife, Josephine Parks, was a quiet-spoken woman, not talkative but easy and mild of speech, a rare practicing Christian. She'd have been one of those strong women in the Acts of the Apostles. What the bosses paid her husband was probably not enough for their groceries (though squirrels, rabbits, quail, fish, and bullfrogs helped quite a bit), but when I ate at their table, whether the dishes were full or half empty, we had a plenty. I remember it as like eating in an Indian household, where the gift of life and friends and relatives is kept quietly in mind, but for non-Indian people it might be clearest if I said it was like that old TV series about the Waltons. Too easy or cheap, though, to compare Mrs. Parks to a sitcom mom. Maybe better to say I have the same feeling when I remember her household as I do when I see a wild turkey or deer or coyote cross the road I'm walking on: hey, the Christians are still not extinct.

I think the most impressed I ever was by how serious they were about religion—they were Assembly of God people—was the Sunday when the tornado came through. I was out in our backyard that day with my slingshot trying to hit a sparrow up in the top of our elm tree there. I had fired my last round pebble and watched it go up, up, slower and slower, till it just lightly tapped the twig by the sparrow's feet where he was chirping with his wings half-opened at the female he wanted to impress, and the sparrow looked kind of surprised and seemed to wonder what had shaken his twig, then turned back to his wooing. So I turned my eyes downward and started to hunt for another pebble, but facing westward toward the wooded hills I saw a funny dark cloud away off west, no bigger than a man's hand as the Biblical phrase puts it, that was kind of bouncing and bumping up and down not far above the horizon there, and when I focused more on the cloud I saw it was black and had a lower part that seemed to reach all the way to the ground. It seemed to be part of a line of clouds there, and as I looked it seemed to be moving in our direction across the hills. My eyes got bigger, because this had been a spring of heavy storms, and in March a tornado had wiped out half the town of Pryor, sixty miles southeast of us. We had no storm-cellar at our house, and the nearest cellar was up at Buck Creek School a mile away. I watched the cloud for a minute or more, thinking this could not really be dangerous it was so small, but I decided to go in and point it out to my folks in the

house. Two of my uncles, Arthur and Bert, were staying with us at
that time, and my stepfather Addison was over in Pawhuska twenty
miles to the west, beyond where that cloud was or seemed to be.
Uncle Arthur, who was quite deaf and refused to wear any of the
heavy-batteried hearing aids then available (this was before transis-
tors of course), was churning butter in the kitchen when I went in,
turning the crank-gears that spun a wooden paddle inside its square
glass two-gallon churn full of heavy Jersey cream. I could see the
cream was a long way from turning to butter, and he was churning
vigorously and did not want to listen as I tried to shout into his ear
my news about this peculiar cloud over to the west. Finally, my
Uncle Bert heard me shouting about it, and he got my mother—also
deaf, though not as hard of hearing as Arthur—and we went into
the west bedroom and looked out its windows. We could see the
cloud had gotten bigger and was still headed in our direction, and
we agreed it looked like a funnel cloud but not too big. Then Uncle
Bert said he wondered what those little specks were that were
dancing around where the funnel touched the ground, and at first
we said it must be birds, hawks maybe, because we thought the
cloud was only a few miles away to the southwest. But then Mom
said she thought that cloud was quite a bit farther off, looked like it
was maybe over near Okesa five or six miles away, and if it was that
far, could we see birds like that, even big hawks?

So my brother Antwine and Uncle Bert and I rushed through
the kitchen past Uncle Arthur churning away, and out into the back
yard where we could get a clear look, and the cloud was still coming
toward us and it was definitely bigger and now looked really almost
black, and we could see the funnel was thick and about halfway up it
along one side a ragged jag of cloud hung down and kind of yo-yoed
up and down without ever touching the ground, while the funnel
just moved steadily toward us from the southwest. Uncle Bert
turned to go back inside, clearly alarmed, and I said, "That's not
hawks, that's trees!" and Antwine said, "Listen, that's not thunder
that's a different kind of roaring." As Bert went in the back door we
heard him yell at Mom to get the car keys and he would round up
the kids, and in a minute he came back out shepherding Maxine and
Josie and Jim and Josephine, and he told Antwine and me to get on

over to the garage and get into the car so we could drive up to the
school and the storm cellar there.

But Antwine wouldn't go. He ran over to the concrete well-
house in our back yard and pulled the manhole cover off and
lowered himself down to stand on the box down there next to the
electric pump with his head sticking out the manhole, and he faced
west where he could watch the funnel-cloud moving toward us, and
he refused to come with Bert and the rest of us toward the garage.
I stayed halfway between wellhouse and garage waiting for Mom to
come out of the house—she had yelled that she could not find the
keys, and she was carrying our baby brother Junior and I could see
her through the bedroom window yanking the drawers out, hunting
the keys. Just then it occurred to me that my cat Squirrelly, and our
dog Tip, were in danger, and I decided to run and get them and load
them into the car. I ran around to the west yard to find them, and
through the bedroom window there I saw Uncle Arthur looking
calmly toward the funnel-cloud, and I motioned at him to come on,
and he just smiled and set the churn on the bureau and kept
churning, and kind of waved at me briefly and said something
which, reading his lips, I thought was "Just a big whirlwind!" So I
ran back around the back, and I saw Tip and Squirrelly crouched
down beside the back porch, and as Mom came by carrying Junior
with the keys in her hand, yelling at Antwine to get into the car, I
picked up Squirrelly in my left hand and got my right arm around
Tip and tried to pick him up. But he pulled away, and I kept
following him across the yard. The wind had begun to blow from
the funnel's direction, furious gusting wind, and I looked up past
the elm tree's tossing branches and saw the black funnel had moved
directly behind Bockius's Hill just west of us but the dark over-
cloud was just above the hill, and it looked as if the funnel would
come up over the hill and right down on us in a couple of minutes
at most. Antwine was standing with head and shoulders out of the
manhole looking intently at the funnel and would not come out.

I managed finally to get an arm around Tip and lift him and
started trying to run toward the car, which Mom had started and
was just backing out of the garage to turn around in the driveway
and head down to the highway for the schoolhouse. But as I ran

toward the car, and came out of the house's lee into the blasting wind which now carried rain and hail, it blew me off my feet and as I fell the dog and cat got free and ran back into the house's lee and through a hole in under the house itself, so I got up and practically flew over to the car, into the door Uncle Bert was holding open, and Mom stomped on the gas and we went jouncing down the lane to the highway. As we went I got one last look westward as the rain and hail blinded us, and I saw the great storm-shape sliding from behind Bockius's Hill and toward the wooded northern rim of the valley, then rain and hail in a solid wall wiped out all viewing in that direction and we drove as hard as possible eastward along the highway to Buck Creek School, passing a car parked just off the highway on the county road leading northward toward where the funnel was headed.

"I think that's Mr. Straw," my mother said urgently, "he must have just been going up to his house."

"Half an hour more and he'd have been in his house, probably just where it's going," Uncle Bert said. The wind now as we drove east on U.S. 60 was blowing directly from the north and nearly taking us off into the ditch, but we made it to the school's driveway, turned off and parked, jumped out and ran through heavy rain around to the cellar, yanked the horizontal door up and open, ran down the steps into the flooded cellar and stood up to our knees in muddy water hoping no centipedes or scorpions would get us. After maybe ten minutes the rain stopped pounding and the wind completely died. We came cautiously out and looked at the clearing skies. There was an odd bluegreen coloring to the cloudless part, this late afternoon in early May, and there were clouds of very different kinds scattered like rags around various parts of the sky, all moving but not in the same directions. As we got into the car again and turned back west toward our house we saw a line of very dark almost black clouds come seething and swirling across from southwest to northeast, in the tornado's wake it seemed, with some of them swooping suddenly upward or around in almost a circle like leaves as they all moved northeastward. I had never seen clouds behave like that.[3]

When we got to the county road where Mr. Straw's brown 1937 Pontiac had been parked, it was gone. Looking north along that road to the rim of wooded hills we could see ragged stumps and edges where the trees had been torn away; evidently the funnel had skirted the rim and headed on further northeast. It was at that point we realized its path seemed directly toward and over the houses of the Parkses and the Straws. We decided to go home first—only a quarter mile further—and then come back and drive north to see if the Parkses and Straws were all right. Back home, Antwine was out and about and told us the details of how the funnel had moved. Tip and Squirrelly came out and I took Squirrelly inside. Nothing had been blown off the house or barns or garage. So we started north along the county road.

As we got up the hill we could look back from its height and see, to the southwest, what looked like the path of a giant lawn-mower, a quarter-mile wide, sheared through the dark green black-jacks for miles over those rolling hills. We knew what to expect before us, where the funnel crossed the road: trees uprooted, hurled every way, snapped off, shattered, strewn. We had to get out and move, drag, turn a few trees, but we could see the tire-tracks where Mr. Straw and his son had made a way for themselves already. At least we knew they had not been caught themselves. But when we got along to where Mr. Straw had built with native sandstone, a year ago, both a house and chickenhouse, only the chickenhouse was standing. Fifty yards away, where the stone house had stood, Mr. Straw and his son Arnold were poking about in the strewn branches and debris. We stopped in their driveway, got out and went over and looked and spoke with them a little. Mr. Straw was a taciturn man who could build or repair anything, and after his first wife had died he had moved here to a small acreage and built this new place, finishing it the previous July just in time to stock its new-set pantry shelves with hundreds of quart jars of produce, fruit, blackberries he had canned himself. It was the loss of this store of home-canned goods that seemed to disturb him most—as if he could easily imagine rebuilding a house (later, he did put a floor into the chicken-house, made room divisions, and lived in it for several years), but

losing all that good food and the jars was a real blow. We did not
stay long there, wanting to get over and see how the Parkses had
fared, but later that summer when I traced the tornado's track I'd
see, every now and then, what must have been shards of those jars
with dried remnants of blackberry preserves still on them, and
thought how the ants had rejoiced at such manna.

But that day we quickly drove on and at the T-junction turned
toward the Parkses' driveway and house. To our vast relief and
surprise the house was untouched, though the storm had mowed
down woods to within a few hundred yards, then turned more
directly eastward and crossed the road to destroy Mr. Straw's house
and goods. Mrs. Parks and the five children were home, Mr. Parks
having been at work over toward Bartlesville—so they had been in
the house, with no storm cellar and no car to try and drive away in,
when they saw the tornado bearing down on them.

"Did you see it coming?" my mother asked.

"Yes, we thought it would hit us," Mrs. Parks said.

"You didn't have a basement or cellar either."

"No, we came out here and knelt down and prayed," Mrs. Parks
said. "The funnel turned just as we thought it was going to come
right over us. It seems the Lord turned his wrath aside for this time."

Later that evening my stepfather Addison and Grandma
Josephine and Aunt Arita came over from Pawhuska, twenty miles
southwest, to see if we were all right, and they told us the tornado
had killed fourteen people on the eastern edge of Pawhuska, missing
Grandma Jump's place south of Pawhuska but hitting Lynn
Addition there before it moved northeast toward us. It barely missed
Osage Hills State Park and the Boy Scout camp, crossed U.S. 60 and
slashed northeast through the Labadie Ranch lands[4] before dipping
down into the Buck Creek Valley and cutting the Dustin Ranch
house in two (they luckily were in Bartlesville just then), then
passed north of Bockius's Hill on the way to the Parks and Straw
houses. From next day's extra edition of the Bartlesville paper we
learned it had passed north of Bartlesville and killed three people in
Dewey, then stayed on the ground for a hundred miles more, up
into Kansas. It was one of the most powerful tornadoes of that

decade in the United States, or so I read years later in a weather-history article on tornadoes; so its missing most of Pawhuska and all of Bartlesville saved at least scores of lives.

When my Uncle Arthur died years later, I kept wanting to write something for him, but couldn't find a way to do it till finally I thought of how he and the Parkses had looked in such different ways at that tornado but with the same kind of calmness, and then I decided that was how I would write about it. Uncle Arthur Camp was a pretty eccentric man, highly intelligent and with a friendly smile, but with a mind like a tree decorated with crepe-paper streamers bearing messages, where even a friendly bird would have to perch and sing rather circumspectly. What he did when the tornado came by in 1942 became a family legend; so when he died, that was the first thing I thought of—that he had just looked a tornado in its lightning-filled eye and gone on about his business. So I wrote of him churning the butter, and us fleeing to the storm cellar, and the Parkses kneeling and praying, as three ways to survive the storms of time. Had he stayed in Oklahoma, instead of moving to California, he might have gone out with more style, but he still, as the chariot went up, would have smiled. The title I've used is a line translated from Dante's *Commedia*—something said by an angel to the pilgrim Dante to persuade him that he should now plunge through the wall of flames to get across from the Mount of Purga-tory, which he has been slowly climbing with Virgil as guide, into the Earthly Paradise where Beatrice will greet him and take him on up into the heavens. I thought of this line, where the angel tells Dante not to be deaf to the beautiful singing over on the other side of that wall of flames, because Uncle Arthur had the same kind of deafness I later developed—caused by otosclerosis, a kind of arthritis of the three little ear-bones—and by 1942 (when the tornado passed by us) he was very deaf, and refused to wear any of the clumsy heavy hearing aids which at that time were all there was for such deafness. So we had to shout loudly to make him hear anything, and were never sure when he actually understood what we were shouting, because he just smiled a pleasant smile and usually went on doing whatever he was doing, no matter what we said.

And Don't Be Deaf to the Singing Beyond

Ed al cantar di là, non siate sorde.
—Angel in Flames to Dante, *Purgatorio* 27.12

You never could tell what my deaf Uncle Arthur heard.
That Sunday when the black storm-cloud came at us,
He sat there churning butter by the bedroom window.
We saw this strange cloud way off west on the hills,
A little dark funnel with specks dancing round it.
"That's only a big whirlwind," he said with a smile.
Well, pretty soon we saw the specks were trees,
We heard this rumble like freight trains on a trestle,
But Uncle Arthur was deaf and wouldn't believe us.
We ran like hell to the car and drove off east—
When hail and rain came blasting after to blind us,
He just sat there in the window, churning away.
Of course the storm passed before we got to the school
And ran down steps to stand in its flooded cellar—
So, wet up to our knees, we drove back home.
When we got in, he had two pounds of butter
All worked, salted, and molded onto dishes.
The funnel had passed a half-mile north and west,
Its swath—a quarter-mile wide of leveled blackjacks—
Went up and over the valley's northern rim.
We drove up north to find out who'd been killed.
Out in the dirt yard of their paintless four-room house
Our Assembly of God friends were standing unharmed.
"We knelt and prayed, God turned his wrath aside,"
Their mother said. Who knows which tasted sweeter,
That Jersey butter from Uncle Arthur's churn,
Or the name of God in Mrs. Parks's mouth?
I still get peeved, thinking of what missed them
So close they saw the lightning up in its blackness,
And what we missed, down in that scorpion-filled cellar.
Well, when my Uncle Arthur died, years later,
A migrant Okie in Porterville, California,
My Aunt Jewell, his brother Woody's wife,

Saw him collapse there with his coronary,
And when she ran up, he lay there on his back,
Turned his eyes to her, smiled, closed them, was dead.
"He was SO deaf," she said, "and he saw my mouth
Just calling and calling, and seemed to think it was funny."

    I hope all this doesn't give the impression that the Parks family
was just goody-goody, all sugar and no spice. There were five kids—
from fair dark-haired Mary Ellen, through Anita with her long thick
blonde braids, husky Walter David, beautiful dark Janey Bell, down
to peachy-blonde Rosalee—and among them they provided plenty
of snips and snails and puppydog tails around house and neighborhood. Mary Ellen was high school age and would soon be married to
Calvin Parker; Anita was in the eighth grade; Walter, my age, was in
the fifth; Janey Bell was in the third; and Rosalee was (I think) in
first grade. A pang shot through me when I first saw Janey Bell's
heartshaped dark face, and I had a crush on her from then on, but
never said a word to her about it. The official reason for my going
up to the Parkses house, when I'd go on my own instead of with
brothers and sisters, was always to chase around the woods with
Walter, but there would always be, as I was walking through the last
bit of woods along the shortcut from the highway to their house, a
hope of seeing Janey Bell just for a minute to ask her if Walter was
there that day. (He might be off in the woods with his cousin
Sammie, or out on the pumphouse rounds with his dad, some days.)
I always presented myself as interested in some other girl, first at
Buck Creek School, then later in Bartlesville schools, and it has to
be admitted that from time to time this was true enough; but not
till I had had my heart broken several times during college, and I
had gone overseas, would the sense leave me that my permanent
romantic interest was Janey, if I could only get up the courage to at
least try and go out with her at last.
    The nearest I actually came to speaking out was after the
Parkses had moved over to Webb City and I occasionally got over,
maybe in the summer of 1946, for two or three days at a time. I
thought maybe Janey showed just a hint of being interested in me
then, and she actually wrote me a letter after one such visit, saying

that things were really dull over there and Webb City was just a wide spot in the road, but I couldn't think what to write her in reply and never managed to answer. It was like one of those machines on which you pull the bar and hope all the spinning symbols will come up the same, all cherries, and they never quite do. For one thing, there was always a lot to be doing with Walter and his Webb City relatives and buddies, at a time when Walter and I were fifteen and some of the other boys wanted more from a girlfriend than romantic looks, and I was trying to keep that kind of crude stuff at a distance from what I privately felt about a girl three years younger than me and serious about her churchgoing. So I spent my time just hanging around with the guys, carefully not looking too much in her direction, afraid I might blush and give myself away, and going along with any kind of mischief we could get up to around Webb City or in the nearby pastures and fields. There was plenty of mischief usually; one time in particular when I was over, some boys talked Walter and me into going watermelon-stealing, and I wrote this up in another piece that came out in *Ponca War Dancers,* which I have called "Chimes at Midnight" because it reminisces about what two old friends got up to when they were a lot younger, the kind of reminiscing that Shakespeare made fun of in the scene between Falstaff and Judge Shallow in *Henry the Fourth, Part 2,* where Justice Shallow keeps trying to claim he was a real hellraiser when they were young—while Falstaff, hoping to get a big loan from him, goes along with him, saying, "We have heard the chimes at midnight, Master Shallow," but then tells his own buddies *sotto voce* that it never really happened like that. This is what I wrote, and some of it is *pretty* close to what really happened:

Chimes at Midnight

Dear Walt,
      Well, that was some weekend. Can't see why Janey Bell
          thinks Webb City is just a wide spot in the road,
            unless she means there's never any news
      because there's no newspaper there to print it.
         Way things went last weekend though, you all

will need a RADIO station before too long.
    I mean, you'll surely have to get a new preacher—
        won't you?—
and let's hope he won't ever preach a sermon
    like the old one did last Sunday morning there.
    Got up there bashing Satan around
    with a two-by-four practically, but got
so worked up he must have forgot himself
      telling what a sinner he was—I never saw
so many surprised husbands all at one time
    as when he got down to details, and all their wives
    just sitting right there, too dumbfounded to lie.
Didn't take that preacher long to run out
    of cheeks to turn, did it, when they got hold of him—
but I expect the carpenters have fixed
    the doors and things back up by now, and if
      he's really gone to California
    I hope the people out there will do
like the preacher says instead of like he does,
    but out there maybe no one will notice.
    —Listen, have you ever heard any more from that old farmer
that tried to kill us with his thirty-thirty?
    I think we ought to prosecute that guy;
    all we were doing was stealing his watermelons,
and Billy never said till afterwards that we were the third
    bunch that got into his patch that day.
I didn't even know, when I came running across that cornfield
    with the big green melon on my head,
that that was his prize one with the orange meat,
    till the thirty-thirty bullet knocked it to pieces and
      the juice ran down my face. Man, it made
      my eyes so sticky that when
    I was trying to sprint on down the ditch
    and ran right over poor little Billy in front of me,
    I never stopped to see how he was doing,
    but I don't think he even noticed.
But why couldn't that farmer just use rock salt in a shotgun?

Him with that rifle, we had to run miles
                          to get out of range,
          along that row of Osage orange trees and out on the prairie,
and even there that big Black Angus bull
                  would've tromped us into mincemeat if we had not
          just got across the pump-rod line in time.
          Well, we found out what stinging nettles are—
and I just hope that farmer tries someday to use a few
                  for toilet paper, the way we did.
There's not much happening, here on this horseless ranch—
          come over, though, and we'll find something maybe,
might run some greyhounds out on the prairie
                          east of Bartlesville—
          there's lots of jacks. Might start a coyote even.
P.S. There's a note for Janey Bell enclosed.
                          Don't open it.

(There wasn't any note for Janey Bell, of course, but maybe she'll
open this one.)

11

Training Greyhounds
Buck Creek to Abilene, 1943–1948

Speaking of running greyhounds, for several years when I was in my teens I helped train greyhounds. A mile west of us, across Buck Creek, a local grocery-owner named Vernie Mikels had a place with some hundred and sixty acres where he had built up a "greyhound farm"—starting with a few dogs in the 1930s, he expanded until by 1947, when I was sixteen, there were a hundred and sixty dogs yelping and racing up and down the chickenwire kennels from their little huts to the gates and back. One of his dogs, Upside Down, had won a national championship in the coursing trials in the 1930s, and when Vernie put him at stud a lot of his pups turned out to be big winners too, so Vernie got more and more enthusiastic and a lot of his store's profits went to the dogs. Vernie lived in town, and he would rent the house and acreage in Buck Creek to a family with the arrangement that the man would take care of the dogs. That was a lot of work, and increasingly so as the number of dogs rose and new kennels were built. To about 1942, the family renting there were the Popes, and their kids were beautiful platinum blond kids with chicory-flower eyes and Malibu tans who could have been from Copenhagen, they looked so Danish. But about that year, Mr. and Mrs. Pope and Lorene and John and the rest departed for some other place, and Mr. and Mrs. Kendall and kids moved in.

Mr. Kendall was lean and hard-muscled as a greyhound himself, but his wife defined the word "buxom," with her ample shape, fair skin and cherry lips and friendly ways; she also was smart academically, did a lot of reading, and was a sharp observer. He had been a champion sprinter at Bartlesville High School, and when they moved into the place they had just the two kids, Johnny—twelve at the time—and his younger sister, not yet in grade school: both blue-eyed blonds, Johnny the image of his father, the girl watching everything quietly a little like her mother. Johnny did not go to school with us at Buck Creek but stayed in the Bartlesville school where he was in the sixth grade that year. Mr. Kendall drove him in every day on his way to work there. He was a house painter by trade, and the first I saw of him he was doing the painting of the new Buck Creek School building that the WPA was finishing in 1942. Only that spring had we moved into the big new stone building, so airy and light and luxurious—before that we had continued schooling in the dark old white clapboard building, with its wood-burning stove and its bell tower at the south end, that had been the first school in the new District 66 after enough people were settled onto the Osage allotment lands around there that a school was thought necessary.

Osages had held out longer than any other tribe against individual land-allotments, and when it was forced upon us we made sure we got all the reservation land allotted to Osage people, instead of settling for only a hundred and sixty acres per family with the rest being declared "surplus" and handed out to non-Indian homesteaders, the way land on other reservations was dealt out. The allotment was made in 1906; then various Osage families chose their lands around the valley, divided it up and sold or leased some to non-Indian families, and people built houses and began to farm or to commute to work in Bartlesville, the oil-boom town five miles to our east, just across the Reservation line in Washington County (where the Cherokee and Delaware tribal holdings had been). Dave Ware, an original Osage allottee, had given the acreage on which the new Buck Creek Rural District 66 School was built about 1915 or so; Dave and Polly Ware lived a quarter mile from us, just across U.S. Highway 60, a mile west of Buck Creek School and a mile east of the Vernie Mikels place where the Kendalls, in 1942, had become the greyhound-managing family.

It was late that spring, I think, that I heard one of the WPA finish carpenters kidding Mr. Kendall about the new set of twins Mrs. Kendall had just had. I liked the way Mr. Kendall grinned and blushed and spoke easily and kindly with those congratulating him. A few days later his yellow van came up our driveway and he asked to buy some of our baled hay to use as bedding for the dogs. He also asked if any of us kids could come and do some work taking care of the dogs. Since we were in tough shape financially, it did not take long to agree that I would be coming up there to help out, for a dollar a day, on weekends; and later I would work also after school during the week, and often on Sunday.

That was the start of several years of occasional work, especially during the two main racing seasons of each year, in fall and spring, when the best dogs were being trained for the national coursing trials held in Abilene, Kansas. Mr. Kendall was a man generous and kind, transparently honest, working himself almost to death for a bare living. By 1948, the twins of 1942 had younger siblings—though their older brother Johnny, without ever saying a word, looked as though he would have preferred to have fewer plates at the table and more food on each. The great success of Mikels's stud dog Upside Down (whose fees must have helped the finances a great deal) had been followed up by buying an Irish champion, Drumhurlin Border—a very beautiful but apt-to-bite big fawn and white dog—whose pups were now moving into the competition with some early spectacular results. So there were kennels to be cleaned, dog-runs to be raked, great vats of food to be cooked, cows to be butchered and their meat ground up, their bones cooked. There was wood to be cut for the fires, there was plowing and harrowing of the coursing-fields. Above all there were dogs to be walked, or raced, or groomed. In September and October, and in April and May, this meant my getting up at five and either waiting for Mr. Kendall to drive up and get me, or sometimes just walking the mile up to their place, so long as I was there near five, to start the walking and maybe to help arrange and carry out the racing competitions. I kept doing this work all through high school, most intensively during my junior and senior years.

When the heaviest training duties were on, Mr. Kendall had to

hire on an extra hand or two for short periods. One year, when I
was about fifteen, Buster was an extra hand, and I have written a
piece about something that happened when he was working with us.
I have called it "Free White and Fifteen," because those words
would apply to him at that time, and I thought with both irony and
truth—because in the old segregated Oklahoma you used to hear
people saying loudly, when they wanted to proclaim their indepen-
dence and freedom to do whatever they damned well pleased, that
they were "free, white, and twenty-one." Buster had anything but an
easy life, yet he had more brains than was good for him, and I have
wondered a lot about what became of him. Here is the poem, which
was published in the Cornell University journal *Epoch* in 1970 and
has been reprinted in *Ponca War Dancers:*

Free White and Fifteen

When the bullet hit, the horse keeled over dead.
The little kids cried that had ridden on him all week,
But hell, he was bought to feed the dogs, not ride on,
Old broken-down plowhorse, gentle or not.
We hitched the tractor, hooked him onto the platform;
John skinned the head, chest mine, Buster the belly,
By then tight-bloated: Buster slit through
And bloof! a spray-spout of bloody piss shot upward
Drenching Buster on face and body and hair.
Well, I broke out laughing and Buster went nuts,
He waved his skinning knife and came after me.
I swung and knocked him back on the flayed ribs,
Knocked down the middle knuckle on my right hand.
He raised up glaring at me for half a second,
Then flopped back flat, eyes rolled up and closed,
Just spread his arms like sleeping and lay dead still.
The smell of piss and blood came back with hand-hurt,
The rush of greyhounds jumping and barking, racing
Each other up and down the kennel fences.
"If you damn fools have had your fun," Johnny said,
"Let's get this horse cut up." I hopped around

On the bloody slippery platform, got my knuckle back,
Then Buster sat up. He didn't recall getting drenched
But after a rest he felt like working again.
We salted, folded the hide, flopped it into a barrel.
We gutted, quartered, carved meat like cherry Jello
In chunks, tossed slivers to favorite dogs.
—That night, Buster and I were going to a movie.
We never got there. His head still hurt. Instead,
We thumbed in to his house, where I'd never been.
His folks weren't there. Hadn't seen them lately, he said,
But they'd turn up and want some of his money
Before too long. He'd drink it up first, enjoy it.
One of these days the old man would wake up
With a butcher knife in his back if he kept taking money.
One room was Buster's. Linoleum cracked, floor warping,
Bare bulb—all over the floor and on the bed
Comic books, pulp Westerns, detective magazines
Open with torn pages, the bed unmade.
He could spend whole days just reading things.
Sometimes all Sunday he wouldn't go out of his room,
Just lay there reading. He could write better
Than some of these guys, was going to rent a typewriter.
—We finally walked downtown and looked around.
Plenty of girls, but hell, they wanted cars
And guys with money. Us, we carried the stink
Of twelve hours' work at lowpaid country jobs,
Nowhere to take them, couldn't even hand out a line
Worth giggling over. Finally I had to get home.
Buster stood waiting while I tried to thumb.
Waited so long we walked across the street
To Old Man Brokeback's stand and snatched two pears—
Had to run like hell. A car finally stopped.
We'd be at work next morning, cleaning kennels.

12

Greyhound Coursing Trials
Abilene, Kansas, 1947

I think the work I most enjoyed was actually walking the dogs.
There was a fenced field we most often walked the dogs around,
each lap a half a mile. I would have in each hand from two to four
dogs on leashes, a total of four to eight dogs, and would walk each
contingent from two to four miles—four to eight laps around the
field. Sometimes, to vary the walk, we would take the dogs up the
highway a mile or so, not so bad in the early dawning, when there
were very few cars and we could hear them or see them coming a
long way off and make sure the dogs were well in hand and we had a
good place to get off the road till the car or truck had passed. On
school days we had to finish the walking before 8:00 A.M., so Johnny
and I could jump in the family car—a 1936 Hudson Eight that had
to be fine-tuned once a week or so to make sure it would start and
get us there—and rumble the six or seven miles in to high school.
Then at three o'clock we had to jump into the car and chug back
out for the rest of the day's work, finishing sometimes well after
dark, which in May would be eight to nine o'clock.

Some of the dogs were being trained for friends of Vernie
Mikels, notably some owners and handlers from Florida and other
places who boarded their dogs and had them trained by Mr. Kendall
and his helpers. We had to make all possible allowances to be sure
these dogs were in peak condition when the owners came in, not so
long before the national trials, or came by for a trial competition,

which would involve getting a number of jackrabbits for the coursing in a large flat field adjacent to the walking-place. Other owners would bring their dogs in pickups with camper-shells, and we might run as many as fifteen or twenty pairs of dogs in competition, a couple of weeks before the national trials were scheduled.

Most people have seen or know what it is like to race greyhounds around a circular track after a mechanical rabbit, but few know how the coursing of live jackrabbits used to be done—it probably has long since been outlawed. I described it in a poem, partly fictional, about the National Coursing Trials in Abilene—which I went to with the Kendalls in fall 1947, racing some of the dogs we had trained, including two of my favorites, a big brindle dog named Osage Border (son of Drumhurlin Border and Osage Sue) and his sister, a little white and brindle bitch named Miss Border. The poem is a sestina, and I did it to see whether, as I suspected, the Hemingway narrative tricks—repeating key words, simplifying language, stripping everything down to sensory fact and the implications to be drawn by alert readers—can be adapted to this impossibly constrained poetic form of the sestina. A sestina has 39 lines: six stanzas of six lines each, and a coda of three. At the end of each line in a given stanza, one of the key words is used, so each of them is used once in a stanza, and a total of six times in the first 36 lines. Then in the three-line coda each of the six words is used once, with two occurring in each of the three lines (one at the end, one toward the middle). The sestina form was probably invented by the troubadours or the trouvères in medieval France and Italy and Spain, and what struck me about most examples of it was how hopelessly arty as well as artificial the writers made it. So I said to myself, Hell, why not actually tell a story, the way Hemingway and Gertrude Stein did, and thereby turn the sestina's weakness (artificial repetition) into a strength (natural repetition as in telling a story)? So I tried it, with this result:

Greyhound Coursing Trials

Osage was coursing against this fawn greyhound,
Fawn Dough, small alert dog with early foot

to spare and quickest one on turns
in the whole Futurity bunch. Osage was fast,
but eighty pounds of clumsy brindle drive
and overgrown feet on turns, so a fast rabbit

and chance for Osage to pass the fawn greyhound
and maybe win the kill with his first drive,
at least get points for leadup and first turn,
was what we hoped for. I went out on foot
with five others picked for running fast—
we formed a V, out from where the rabbit

would be let loose, to shoo him straight and fast:
"Haaah, JACK!" The rabbit leaped and now the greyhounds
broke from their slips; I heard through the slapping drive
of their feet Osage whimper, behind by a foot
when they passed me, but the rabbit wouldn't turn
till past our shouts, and Osage turned the rabbit

then lunged on wide; Fawn Dough cut through the turn
and then just COURSED, nose not more than a foot
behind bobbing tail, back and forth too fast
and close for Osage to cut in and drive
for the kill, but the jack led both greyhounds
straight at the fence; full speed they and the rabbit

crashed into yielding wires; Osage untangled fast,
with head up looked wildly round for the rabbit—
near him, hopping dazed away from greyhounds
towards the escapes, unsteady and slow of foot.
The two dogs lunged, Osage showed most drive
and picked it up clean before it could turn.

I ran over, snatched it dangling from the greyhounds,
snapped leash on Osage, saw he favored one foot,
cleaned fuzz from his throat, held up the rabbit

for judges to see from their stand, carried him fast
out through the gate onto the graveled drive,
set him gently on grass, straightened and turned

when Johnny came hollering up the drive as fast
as a greyhound, yelling "He won! killing the rabbit
won it!" till he saw, as I turned, the ruined foot.

13

Okie Survival

My cousin Roy Camp was one of the better watermelon-stealers in our part of the country, between Pawhuska and Buck Creek—or at least he told the best stories about when the farmers really DID use rock salt in the shotgun, and he once went around for days unable to sleep on his back or even sit down because he got peppered with some of it one afternoon. Sixty years later, when I was out in California visiting with him and his family, we got to talking about some of those good old bad old days, so after I was back in St. Louis, in June 1996, it was time to write this book for Roy, who as is said in the poem had taught me to read back in 1936. He had lived with us that whole year, out in the Buck Creek Valley, because not long before his father had been beaten to death in the Pawhuska jail (Roy had tried to pull the policemen off as they dragged his father through the doors). When his mother remarried, Roy did not at first like the new stepfather; so the year my twin sister and I started to Buck Creek School he lived and went to school with us.

Three years later—as Steinbeck was writing *The Grapes of Wrath*—Roy and a buddy hopped a freight train and rode out to California to join his mother and stepfather at a sawmill near Truckee, up by Lake Tahoe. A few years later he married a good strong woman, served in the Marines in World War Two, then saw to it that his mother Loretta had a good house right near where he and Celestine located in Porterville. When I visited them for Roy's seventieth birthday and went down to the local mall for a birthday dinner, we couldn't move twenty feet along a sidewalk or an aisle without people greeting him with a big grin and handshake or hug. So when I wrote this I wanted to remind Welfare Kings like certain governors and presidents that the food on their table is put there not only by "immigrants" but also by "natives"—people looked down on by those in power, even as they hand rich contributors largesse from the banks and businesses and porkbarrels made possible by the Okies, Indians, Chicanos, Koreans, Blacks, Hmongs, Vietnamese, and probably even a few capitalistic Brits and Ayrabs and Noo Yawkers out there in LaLaLand.

Winning the Dust Bowl

There was a reaching up
into the dusty leaves after
the biggest most golden ones, and almost
falling off the ladder—stretching up into
the stiff pungent leaves, on through
dead twigs, brushy branches where my fingers
just barely touched, touched and tipped
a heavy orb till with one last touch it
dropped upon my palm—
deep gold with greeny tinges, warm to fingers
closing despite the ladder's shaking—
and then a turning cautiously on rungs to toss
that last tree-ripened navel orange into
the sure and waiting hands below
of my cousin Roy—
                    and the climbing down
to the solid loamy ground of his back yard
behind the house he built at the edge
of Porterville, by now just fringing the upper
middle class's brick and well-coiffed
development houses built over orange groves
and olive trees where as he says
if he and Celestine could have saved a little more from
their migrant Okie labor up and down this Gold Rush State
and further, from the Salton Sea's tomatoes all the way up

to Oregon's cherries, Washington's apples, all that
stoop labor, ladder aches, labor camps, sometimes
our Ponca cousins working alongside—as he says,
a little more in the savings bank and maybe
some twenty acres bought at the edge of Porterville
when land was still dirt cheap
would have made him a millionaire where now the bankers,
lawyers, heads of businesses live, as well as the doctor
from Pakistan who diagnosed his pancreatic cancer—but then
what's in THEIR yards is ornamental, flowers briefly,
looks beautiful but not for eating, what's on
their tables grows on some other field
of earth where Others work, and here
are these tree-ripened oranges, navels and
Valencias, in Roy's back yard. I can't wait, we peel
and eat two big ones bursting with juice
and sweetness, then we wipe our hands
and mouths and he puts
into a plastic grocery bag two dozen dusty globes
for me to take back down to Pasadena, and walking back
toward the house we stop for onions,
enormous purple ones he's just dug up,
we find some ties and string the onions up to dry,
we look at the green tomatoes in their mini-jungle there
in his garden plot, the peppers, okra just poking up,
see where small apricot and peach trees now have bloomed,
and then past his window cooler that he built
and hooked up specially to a backyard hydrant here
(last night, cool breezes from it helped me sleep),
we see the huge rose-tree still in bloom and he pauses there
before its great crimson depths and fragrance and says quietly
that this was given by a friend before he died
who said he hoped that when it bloomed
they'd have good thoughts of him,
which, as Roy said, they surely do, and then
Celestine came out the front door past the amaryllis
with its humongous scarlet blooms and we walked

to my car, opened the trunk and flumped
the oranges in their plastic bag into its depths and slammed the lid
and we hugged and said we hoped
that next year on his seventy-second birthday
we'd have some more strawberries over angelfood
with whipped cream like Celestine had just fixed for us—
"You realize, Mike," he'd said,
"these aren't my strawberries—we
bought those a couple blocks away at that fruit stand
in the corner of that big strawberry field,
three dollars for what seems like half a bushel
from that Hmong family who run the stand—if all
those Hmongs the government's bringing in here now
would work like them I'd never object
to all the government's doing for them
and never did for us."
                       So we had talked a little
about Viet Nam, and what we owed
the people we had used to kill and save our empire,
and what the Okies of the Dust Bowl times,
Roy and Celestine and our families,
had done for California—but now
when I closed the trunk-lid and we hugged
and said good-bye for this year and who knows
how long, it wasn't Hmong and Okie,
Mexican, Black or Indian, but just the three of us now—
a cousin like an older brother who'd taught me to read
in the first grade,
the beautiful woman he had married
when he had joined the Marines and might have gone
down on Tarawa in the South Pacific,
and me, the academic Osage Okie out for a visit.
"Now listen, Mike," Roy said, and I could tell
my getting lost in a *different* way,
each time I came to Porterville, was on his mind,
"the only thing you have to do to reach the highway
is turn right, right down where I'm pointing,

and follow that all the way." And so I did,
never got lost and drove right down
past orange groves, English walnuts and olives,
past Bakersfield and oilwells pumping,
down Highway Ninety-Nine with its rose azalea blooming, on
into Pasadena where I had some work
on medieval manuscripts to do
at the Huntington Library, on that huge estate
the railroad magnate bought when land
was dirt cheap, built his mansion there, acquired
the Earl of Bridgewater's manuscripts and planted
a lot of cactus, made a Japanese Garden,
a Shakespeare Garden, built
an Art Museum, made a big Foundation—
or should I say he hired
a lot of workmen and they did it for him? It may have been
on Mister Huntington's railroads that my cousin Roy
was riding, in or under boxcars, four years after his dad
was beaten to death in the Pawhuska jail, and Roy
rode freezing out to California and made a way
to put good food on many tables and to build
a family, house, a life with friends, children,
grandchildren, fellow fishermen who laugh and know
what it's like to catch
and let them go, and stretch the truth only
enough to make it credible.
Meanwhile, for academics the Huntington's
a gorgeous place to work, whole gardens full
of roses named for people who all hope
we'll have good thoughts of them when they bloom,
and there are many Friends of the Huntington
who surely do.

14

Transubstantiating

Even as a kid I saw watermelons as among the world's wonders, and
very little was more astonishing to me than watching the vines grow
where we or somebody else had planted a few seeds in "hills"—how
they grew, and sent out their vines, and the yellow mealy blossoms
came onto them, and then the little cucumbery melons appeared
where the blossoms were, and swelled and stretched out, and finally
rounded into the big green melon we could thump and thump and
at last decide was ripe enough to pick, and ice down, and take out to
the back yard and carve up on the concrete of the well-house, and
break out dripping pieces to eat in a summer twilight. But melons
did not grow well on the soil of our garden where we lived in Buck
Creek; the best ones grew down in the creekbottoms where families
lived way back from the highways and gravel or dirt roads.

At any rate, we didn't always steal them, and sometimes we
actually paid money for them. Sometimes there would be old beatup
trucks that would come lumbering eastward along U.S. 60 with fruit
for sale: bushels of peaches, or great loads of watermelons. I got to
thinking one time about those, and remembering back when we
might buy a bushel of peaches, how very different one peach might
be from another. You'd have a whole bushel to choose from, and one
would be soft, fragrant-sweet, another hard and still acidly green,
though each looked blooming ripe. As I was remembering those
trucks one time I got to thinking how it is so different now when we
almost always just go in to a supermarket for melons, so kids grow

up mostly never seeing things grow and become themselves, and there is no reason to understand that other people are with us in this great natural conspiracy to turn the earth into food fit for angels to go slumming for. So I wrote a piece called "Communing Before Supermarkets" as another way to suggest that getting together for something grown locally used to be possible, though it may hint too strongly that bread and wine and Christianity are not the only ways to transubstantiate the earth.

Communing Before Supermarkets

—It's probably because we were always trying
to have enough money to eat
that I can taste and smell the truckloads
of summer that came by and sometimes
turned jouncing up the long
dirt lane from U.S. Sixty to our house—
they saw kids swarming out in the yard,
white house with a green roof and a big white
two-story garage, haybarn and cowbarn,
nothing around but meadow, no crops, no
rows of corn or hills of watermelons, a lot of hungry kids
that would be wanting what they were taking round
from their truck farms or orchards—
elephantine loads of melons, sometimes the light
green long ones, the striped ones, the dark
green cannonballs, incredible abundance,
or old swaying trucks loaded with bushels of peaches,
apples and apricots, with grapes and pears that I
remember. I wonder, now, where they came from—
over in Sand Creek Valley by the little town
in the Osage Hills, the hamlet really,
they called it Okesa where we
drove once: there we saw a hillside full
of orchards, berry bushes, the sandy bottomland shaggy
with watermelon vines where the great green melons rounded

heavy and warm on the loam—
it struck me staring from the car, how strange
that dirt does turn into their sweet crisp red flesh
and juice in the mouth, that those long vines
can draw the dark earth up and make it melons, and I said
to myself, how does the seed know to make
a watermelon and not an apricot? Then we had brought
our dimes and pennies for a summer's day, we took
the silver and the copper and we turned
them into two huge melons that the blond boy went casually
out into the field and pulled, just those we wanted,
he took our thirty cents and we—
I think we drove away back down to Sand Creek and in
the pebbly shallow ford we drove out in the water and killed
the engine and we took
the melons from the trunk and in the shallow ripples splashed
each other and the car, we washed the car, the melons,
we took them out onto the bank and sat
on a blanket spread across the grass and stuck
a great long butcher knife into the first green melon and it split,
it was so ripe it cracked almost before the knife
could cut it open, the red heart
looked sugar-frosted, dewy with juice and the pieces
broke to our fingers better than to knives,
in the mouth crisp and melting fragrant, spicy nearly,
as pieces of rind were scattered the ants reporting mountains of
manna climbed and swarmed and buried themselves in our leavings
as we stripped to shorts and underthings and waded down into
the deeper colder pool below the ford where the springs
welled slowly out from under the bouldery bank
at the bend, and swimming I thought,
now the melon is turning into me, and my sisters and brothers,
my mother and father and uncles and aunts and into the
ants feasting there on the melon-rinds,
and into the grass and the trees growing there, and into the dirt—
and Sand Creek is turning, this day is turning to night, so now

when we go home I'll remember and it will be turned
into words, and maybe sometime
it would all grow again a long way off, a long way into
the future, and that's what a few pennies and dimes can do
if you have them, a few seeds, a little rain where creekwaters rise,
and the whole world turns into food for all
the different beings in their times.

15

In the Suburbs

I don't want to imply that all good things are out in the country and in childhood. I live in a suburb and a few years back noticed that a lot of other beings live there too, not only finding it a good place but singing about it, which led to writing this next piece, "Given." It is (as mentioned) a suburban poem, set in the block of Pershing Avenue where I live in St. Louis. I tend to wake in the dawn, and on rare occasions get out for a walk in the early and shadowless light before sunrise, when birdsong is just beginning, especially from robins and cardinals. When the leaves are still new and delicate, on the sidewalk I may see a broken blue half of a robin's egg, and look up to hear in those high branches the nestlings hatched and cheeping. And if I go out by night I may hear, under moon and stars among those same branches, the little tree-frogs ululating and chorusing as loudly as, in later summer, the cicadas will be. Song-homes, that's what the trees are, for the small birds or cicadas with wings and the tree-frogs with none, and if I listen they tell me how the world is given to all these beings who sing for their suppers.

Where I have lived since 1976, just across from Washington University where I taught, the houses are mostly two-story brick, and the trees colonnade and arch over the long east-west streets, perfect examples of how perspective converges to a point between the tall solid trunks and airy greens of sycamore and ash and pinoak, redoak and maple, tulip and linden and a locust or two, with dogwood and pine and a blue spruce here and there. I was struck one morning with how the creatures live among the leaves, how they have such abundance there, how the trees have grown up and built their homes for them, how they can all look down on us and hardly ever be noticed by the humans passing beneath, unless they choose to sing or caw or bluejay themselves just to show us who really owns the suburb and its trees.

They live there with the sun and the moon and stars, the waters come down from heaven for them, the bird-transporting wind comes by more promptly and often than our cars or jetplanes, the humans keep planting more trees as the old ones give way. All the hum and buzz and birdsong, squirrel-chatter and flirt of tails and the night's chorus of tree-frogs among the stars and fireflies, the morning's brilliance of butterflies and swellings of oak-galls around those tiny new beings, rappa-tap-tap of woodpeckers, tin flute of robin and the wren's tiny trill, all this alive and aswarm above the clopping sidewalks and rumbling fuming streets every day and night, a whole green world just over our heads among the blue sky and clouds, or just between us and the Milky Way, a world given to its beings as ours is given to us, however we fight over and foul it up.

And we, our bodies are given us as the world we inhabit is given, we come into our cages of molecules and find them built specially for beings of song and flight as much as for the plodding walkers of asphalt paths that we also are, our senses unfurl like new green leaves into a world where brightness falls from air into our selves and we lift up voices, come rain or come shine, to meet its brilliance of dawn and sunset, glare of noon and glitter of midnight. So noticing where we are and how we are in the world, we may try to give thanks for what has been given, maybe leave a few words for the children coming on, in praise of this green world halfway to heaven and just above our heads.

Given

this world to grow into, I know
they'll repossess it shortly, along with
what's left of me—yet, rumpled
into this small pocket of time, I wish
there were a little more of me to sing

the mortgage payments—how it really
dawns on me this morning as
the light has brimmed and spills all rosy into
the east with robins paying
their rent in song and with the downy
woodpecker's telephone-pole tattoo explaining
the nod of daffodils and endless
pinoaks, maples, ash and sycamore and locusts,
sweetgum dogwood and redbud bowing under this
April windstream over
us blind and flightless creatures blundering
noisy and slow as brachiosaurs, squeaking and rumbling
like humpback whales beneath quick birds where they
are singing that the springing wealth of new
leaves and light and flowers has made it
practical to consummate the mystery of
nesting, if
within earshot the right females would return
the secret signs that they will partner them.
We see, we *learn*
to see and hear and feel, the way
those leaves come out of buds all tight
with liquid virtue rising from earth-blind roots
into bright air to fan
their soft translucent green as
they ask the light into their bowers
of sugars, starches, lignins, as we see
in green and hear in song how light
becomes a tree and holds
the singers in its branches where curving
and blue as sky small eggs will open
and blind reptilian robins fledge and find how
to sing the light back into dawn,
their arias and duets soaring above starsongs
of tree-frogs in the summer dark, just as
into translucent salmon sunrise the stars
dissolve, white clouds set sail across

the blue dazzle above us walking on
our stony earth where clopping
and grating we look up into
those heavens of green and blue and white where the trees
without moving are given the earth and
the sun and the stars, and those who have wings now
are singing and those who have climbed
from sea to earth and air and live now on dew and the tree's
plenty are singing where the moon brings back
a softer light from the sun, where the stars bring us the great
glittering darkness that has no end.

16

Noah's Dove

And then there are other aspects of civilization that seem remarkable; I have celebrated one of these in a less formally structured kind of riddle, this time spoken by a jetplane. It amazes me that we can now fly better than the Homeric gods, and see farther than Zeus from Olympos, but take this for granted. Flight has become, to most of us who fly, the most boring miracle of modern times. The great transporting angels have become hotel lobbies. We step into this lobby with our baggage, we sit down and doze or talk with people in the next seats who may be from the Antipodes or from the next suburb to ours, we eat what is so far the most inedible food as yet discovered on earth, we watch an old or new movie or we listen to old or new songs through small machines, and presently we step out of this boredom into a foreign country with a whole new climate and language and dress-code, different food and surprisingly similar vices and virtues, plants and birds and people we have never seen, all delivered to us by courtesy of that boring hotel-lobby magic we have just endured for six or eight or twenty hours or so.

So I have imagined the great silver bird as an Ark, lifting us up onto the flood of air and letting us down in the redeemed world we imagined. Only the most terrible forces and powers can create a shape of profoundly simple beauty; only the brutal abrasion of a tornado could have shaped the silver bullet of a jetplane to slay the Werewolf of Same Old Self, then resurrect it as Prince of Another Country. But I have tried to gentle the mix of miraculous and commonplace, and to keep its monstrous cousins asleep, in this poem. The Riddle of the Stealth Bomber, however, is yet to be written.

Jetliner from Angel City

Earthborn of white
Titanium sand in Magnesium shell from
the foamy sea, I stretch forth from
their silver ark long wings hung
with four hells driving heavenward my
Cave of Vulcan where frozen
chicken boogies high with microwaves over
a shimmer of crimson cloud for a gym-floor, high
over the Mother Of Snowy Wrinkles with all
her dark pines, bears, mountain lions, the
Grand Canyon's sliding silence,
among faint stars around full moon, high
over a neon-jeweled octopus raping the seashore as
I cocoon in home and history strangers hurtling
to China, to Peru, to Inner Space where the
moon is white gold among snowbank clouds over
rivers, oceans, volcanoes,
time-warps ahead and behind us, looking down on
Greenland's icy mountains, pyramids
of San Francisco, Chicago, Cairo, Chichén Itzá,
step in from Siberian winter,
walk out to Samoan summer—
Ah folks, this is your Captain speaking.
Notice that flight of swans
or whooping cranes passing below,
and over there a spectacular
thundercloud's charcoal and salmon castle
gold-lit by swarms of lightning bugs
laid on especially for our flight—
next week we race this century's last
total eclipse's shadow into night, today we're just
your silver dove returning to the earth.

17

In the Hour-Glass
Mundane Mystery #2

The first time I read in a chemistry book that glass is liquid crystal I was astonished, and still am, though I realize plastic has its talents too. I wrote "Liquid Crystal Thoughts" in St. Louis, after I had gone and got a new pair of glasses, and was thinking about how much it means to be able to go on seeing clearly after age fifty. Were it not for bifocals I'd have had to stop reviving manuscripts and watching birds, and the whole world would turn, speak only to others, and leave me out of its conversation.

But glass doesn't just enchant us through itself and into the world. When Stella and I got to Venice in November 1996 and walked through all those canal-crossed streets, in window after window we saw the light from that grey and rainy day leap and dazzle and flow in more shapes and colors than the real world could possibly hold but does.

Liquid Crystal Thoughts

Looking through windshields at sixty-three
years in a seventy-year zone,
I see how this liquid crystal—invented by
volcanoes often, Egyptians somewhat later—
helps us gaze into our age; I see
these beads were WORTH Manhattan maybe, see

glass pluck and cobbler
dark-shining galaxies, brush time away to make
some quasar from a billion years ago
shine freshly in the barrel of our scopes—
see how it gives
champagne a shape and freedom to
send up its bubbles into hearts, and
how acidly the Hasselblads
etch time into our faces—
glass takes us into Amoeba's private lives,
makes Japanese characters Shinto through
its tiny glintzy tubes
into St. Louis,
puts Christmas onto rootless trees,
holds flowers (compare the way earth holds them by the roots)
in water, dying, lets us say
have a glass, not have a plastic—
corrects our visions,
fends off passes,
glass-harmonicates,
swings from the ceilings letting candles
make recreation out of procreation and calls it
chandeliers—is liquid
crystal reality, amazing
the physicists one more time. And sharp;
that insulating stuff which kept us warm,
glass wool they called it, would cut
us to pieces everywhere inside
and so is banned. Look at a gob
twirled on its rod, glowing golden
honey for Hephaestos, and then
the human breath goes in,
the vase will hold
all Venice, Titian's colors and the sea.

18

Song and Dance and Honeybees

In the summer of 1996 the National Endowment for the Humanities
sponsored an eight-week seminar, held at the Hebrew University in
Jerusalem. Its topic was "The Adam and Eve Narrative and the
Christian and Jewish Tradition," which dovetailed perfectly with
Stella's research and teaching, so she applied, was one of twelve
scholars accepted, and in June flew to Jerusalem for the seminar.

I had just been given an October 1996 residency at the
Rockefeller Center for Research and Conferences in Bellagio, Italy,
to finish a book of essays *(Family Matters, Tribal Affairs)*—and, as
it turned out, to begin *this* book—and was invited to give a series
of poetry readings in Italy that November. Both Stella and I also
needed to use library and archival facilities in England—she to
finish her *Milton and the Tangles of Næera's Hair* (University of
Missouri Press, 1997) and continue work on her study of Pindaric
poetry in the Renaissance, and I to keep chasing a scribe and his
patrons around medieval Ludlow.

Our universities kindly gave us leave to hunt these unicorns
during the fall semester. So we arranged that I would fly to
Jerusalem at the end of her eight weeks there, and we would get a
couple of weeks of July/August vacation time: a weekend in
Jerusalem, then a cruise from Haifa up to Rhodes, Cyprus, Patmos,
and Athens. We had expected to spend a few days in Greece, but in
Athens Stella noticed that there were ferries going daily to Crete,
and on impulse we bought tickets, so we had a week on that beautiful island—after which it was back to Athens, wandering around the

Acropolis in the early morning before other tourists flooded in, losing my wallet to a pair of very clever pickpockets, catching a bus from Athens to Corfu and a ferry to Brindisi, where we stayed in a flophouse and pushed away the small-hours drunk who tried to break into our grimy cell. Then we made a Purgatorial journey by rail through Rome and Milan, through Switzerland in a cold midnight to Paris in a rainy dawn. There we paused to recuperate before taking the Chunnel to England and going on to Oxford, where we had leased an apartment for our library-time in August and September—after which we would get back to Italy for the residency in Bellagio and the poetry-reading tour.

We ended up staying in Paris two days, because when we telephoned to confirm our Oxford apartment-lease there were serious glitches that had to be dealt with, and it was easier to deal with these by telephone and fax from Paris, where we could recover from the train-journey, not only with croissants for consolation, but with the fun of chasing after tickets to a Verdi production at the Paris Opera, as well as looking into possibilities at the Opéra Garnier. As it happened, we did get tickets to *Rigoletto* at the Pompidou, but there was nothing going to be on at the Opéra Garnier at times possible for us. As we were coming out of the building disappointed, I was just behind Stella and, with my glasses off, saw on the back of her coat what I thought was a piece of greyish lint, which I reached out to brush away. The lint, however, turned out to be a honeybee, which ran its stinger into the ball of my thumb. I dropped the bee, carefully pulled the stinger out without squeezing the venom-sac, and sucked the thumb all during our walk across the Seine and back to the hotel. There was plenty to distract us from bee-stings—one distraction being the sudden recall of something in *Le Monde* which told me why that bee was there.

Passing a kiosk that morning, I had bought the newspaper to see whether the world was still going to hell in a handbasket, and found that it was. But there was one lovely feature piece in *Le Monde* that day: a report that on top of the Opéra Garnier building there was an apiary, whose owner had given not just a surprising account of why he had set the hives there, but a tale of what the clever bees had got up to that nearly put him out of business. He put the hives up there, said the beekeeper, because he realized there were more flowers in Paris than in country meadows and orchards—flowers for every season, cared for by gardeners and park-keepers, so his bees always had plenty of nectar from exotic blooms, and they made more honey, with more exquisite flavor, than the bees in hives he set out in orchards and fields.

But, the beekeeper said, not all was rose and mimosa: not long ago, he confessed, honey from the Opéra Garnier hives had begun to taste very strongly of vanilla. His customers complained loudly, and the beekeeper had to track the flight of his bees to find out where the vanilla was coming from. He did not have to go far: in an ice-cream shop down a neighboring street, the bees had discovered that the lids were left off some large containers of vanilla sirup, and were loading up on this with great enthusiasm. A word to the wise, and the container-lids were put tightly on, the bees returned to their nectar-gathering, and the wax cells were full again of innocent honey.

This more than made up for a throbbing thumb. So then I began remembering how, wherever Stella and I had been walking lately, there had been the bees—honeybees larger or smaller, bumble-bees with yellow or gold-and-white rumps—in the herbs on the hills in Jerusalem where we walked that Sabbath before we caught the cruise ship, in the dry fields of the old Greek shrines on Cyprus headlands, in the fruit-market on Rhodes, high up on Patmos in the Aegean, around the Acropolis, on the sunlit mountains in Crete, and here in the soft rain of Paris.

Then I remembered that fragmentary line attributed to the poet Sappho, a line of which Stella was fond and that she had quoted (in Greek, which she translated for us) in 1975, when we were driving around Greece in a Volkswagen and found a lovely small beach-hotel down at the tip of the Pelion peninsula, after passing through uplands fragrant with the herbs and flowers where, when we pulled off to drink from a spring-fountain, the bees were humming. "Neither the honey nor the honeybee," the line said: only that, and of course we are left to wonder what the poem was of which this line was a part, and whether its honeybee was the Mother Goddess, a special friend of Sappho, or an *Apis mellifera*. Muses, I thought: everywhere we've wandered, this summer, is where the Muses haunt—and with that I remembered those lines in the most moving (to me) of all Milton's poetry, his invocation to the Muse at the beginning of Book Three of *Paradise Lost*.

What's touching is that after Milton has begun with such grandeur ("Hail, Holy Light"), speaking in epic fashion to the Divine Light which was the first-born child of Heaven when God created the world, he is humbled by remembering that he himself is utterly blind, unable to see the Light to which he calls. He speaks then of what it is like to be blind, saying to the Holy Light:

> thee I revisit safe,
> And feel thy sovereign vital lamp; but thou
> Revisit'st not these eyes, that roll in vain
> To find thy piercing ray, and find no dawn;
> So thick a drop serene hath quenched their orbs,
> Or dim suffusion veiled. Yet not the more
> Cease I to wander where the Muses haunt,
> Clear spring, or shady grove, or sunny hill,
> Smit with the love of sacred song; but chief
> Thee, Sion, and the flowery brooks beneath
> That wash thy hallowed feet, and warbling flow,
> Nightly I visit: nor sometimes forget
> Those other two equalled with me in fate,
> Blind Thamyris and blind Mæonides,
> Tiresias and Phineus, prophets old—
> Then feed on thoughts that voluntary move
> Harmonious numbers, as the wakeful bird
> Sings darkling, and in shadiest covert hid
> Tunes her nocturnal note.

Yet even those words were not enough to bring Milton out of his personal darkness. He can continue to "wander where the Muses haunt," to recall, in darkness, shining words from classical poetry and Biblical prophecy and song, and the hope still lives in him to achieve in English, as the Muse dictates to him, a poetry as magnificent and lasting as that of Homer and the ancient prophets:

in darkness he sings, like the nightingale, what is given him to sing. Even so, there comes down upon him again the sense of how much is lost with eyesight, how great a part of his world:

> Thus with the year
> Seasons return, but not to me returns
> Day, or the sweet approach of even or morn,
> Or sight of vernal bloom, or summer's rose,
> Or flocks, or herds, or human face divine—
> But cloud instead, and ever-during dark,
> Surrounds me, from the cheerful ways of men
> Cut off, and for the book of knowledge fair
> Presented with a universal blank
> Of nature's works, to me expunged and razed,
> And wisdom, at one entrance, quite shut out.

What seems to me most poignant is that in listing here the things most missed in his blindness, Milton names as last and greatest loss the "human face divine." The very first thing a baby learns to recognize is the face of its mother or father; for humans, facial recognition is basic to the very sense both of identity and of community—and to be unable to see the faces of other humans is surely one of the hardest things about going blind. That is why Milton has put it last—and he adds the adjective "divine" because he believed that God made humankind in his own image, so that losing the human face is like losing the near presence of God.

But this is John Milton, who will not surrender:

> So much the rather, thou, celestial light,
> Shine inward, and the mind through all her powers
> Irradiate: there plant eyes, all mist from thence
> Purge and disperse, that I may see and tell
> Of things invisible to mortal sight.

I have to admit, it's a long way down from Milton's epic magnificence to the more or less pastoral verse into which that

Parisian bee-sting had driven me—so I had better say something like "Return, Alpheus: the dread voice is past / That shrunk thy streams...." Shrunken or not, here is the poem in question:

Where the Muses Haunt

Neither the honey nor the honeybee
—a fragment from Sappho

Atop the Opéra Garnier in Paris there's
an apiary, lots of beehives where
the bees make honey from the flowers
of all the parks and gardens in that City of Light—
the keeper of those bees has said the honey's finer
than from his hives in the countryside
because Paris has so many exotic
flowers where the bees can gather
nectar and pollen, sweet as though from
Manet and Renoir paintings of *la vie en rose,* fragrance of
blossoms in the Jardins de Luxembourg, the Tuileries,
from windowbox and lindenbaum,
orangeries, and why not roses around the tombs
of Baudelaire, Ronsard, and Mallarmé—or, for all
that music hived in l'Opéra Garnier,
the graves of Massenet and Gounod?

And high up on Mount Ida there were small bees
on those dry herbal thorns, humming
and gathering where goldfinches flitted,
when we were looking (like Saturn) for
the Dictæan Caves where Zeus was born
and the Curetes howled to drown his wawling—
and down in Minoan vales new cicadas
were singing over the great ruined palaces
of Knossos, and those of Phaistos,
as tourists wandered quietly under pines
stepping on baked hard earth with its holes
where those Muses' Daughters

after their seventeen dark years had come up
to sing in the pines over the ragged rooms
of the Blue Dolphins and the Dancing Ladies—
one of whom came up
to take our orders as the waitress
in our seaside hotel that night, her profile and
her dark hair's curls and ruby smile
exactly theirs, at seventeen.

On Sion Hill, one sunlit Sabbath, its fragrant herbs
were full of white-rumped bees, humming too around the silent
Tombs of the Patriarchs, and two days later high
on that Cyprus sea-cliff where among broken columns
of Apollo's temple butterflies were floating—nymphs
and satyrs, naturally—

and then we were whisked
zigzagging in a Mercedes taxi up and up
on the Isle of Patmos to the monastery with St. John's
pillow of stone and its gold-and-incense relics of
his *Revelation*—though what got to me
was a cobalt bay with white cruise ships waiting beside
the town's cafes and tourist shops under
a sky of luminous blue with two peregrine
falcons hovering, quick wingbeats ready
to tower and stoop like meteors into the flight
of white doves veering panicky over orange roofs—but then
the falcons circled and winged away,
the doves spiraled out and back over
the harbor's blue, and waiting
for the taxi to take us down again the bees
went on with their gathering from the pale blue
rosemary and from thyme.

19

Bellagio Time

In November 1996, after Stella and I had been given the rare grace of a month in Bellagio by the Rockefeller Foundation people, so I could work on this book among other things, some days she might leave her laptop to view an Alp or museum, or go hear an opera in one of the nearby towns. Being naturally a virtuous and hardworking person, I kept my nose at the grindstone, and sitting in that room, looking out at the Paradisal view of gardens terracing down to Bellagio by the azure lake under sunlit mountains beyond, I thought it was time to celebrate some of the other beings who had been lately keeping me awake at night. Earlier that year, I had been reading Alexander Skutch's *Life of the Hummingbird*, about the "courtship or singing assembly" found in many species (reminds me of the medieval Puy in Flanders and England especially—Juliet Vale's *Edward III and Chivalry* I think has accounts of this). Then in November, winding up that month's work at Bellagio, I was going through computer files of summer correspondence and again read what Skutch (p. 61) says: "Some of the hermits and the green violet-ears sing tirelessly all day long, with such intensity that they appear to be highly efficient machines for transmuting nectar into squeaks. Some of these all-day singers interrupt their recitals only long enough to wet their throats with nectar from the nearest flowers and to chase trespassers. They spend about as much of the day at their singing stations as an incubating female of their kind does on her eggs." Creating new hummingbirds is more wonderful than composing squeaksongs, but evidently neither happens without the other:

could be that's why Muses matter. It seems also that it is not always the male who sings: "the rufous hermit of South America sticks out his long white tongue toward the female, who warbles sweetly while watching him display before her." Sounds like Amneris and Aida with Radamès ("Ritorna Vincitor!"). But I was most enchanted by Skutch's praise of "the exquisite little gem of the Guatemalan mountains, the wine-throated hummingbird, whose sweetly varied outpouring continues for the better part of a minute. If only it were a little more forceful, it might win for its author a place among the world's renowned songsters." (Ah, Emily!) I wondered whether a CD, "Songs of the Wine-Throated Hummingbird," would make the humpback whale move over—or maybe we could arrange a duet, humpback whale and wine-throated hummingbird.

So of course I had been hoping to write about this, and one November morning, with Stella off to Lugano to dip her toes in Switzerland, and I having nothing more beautiful to look at than Como in its grey silken négligée of rain and mist, and the mountains sliding ermine stoles of cloud over their décolletage, there was time to tap into the silicon's sapphire and gold lightning this Fabergé plot for the whales and hummingbirds to hatch. I should add that it owes considerable also to the pleasure of hearing music presented by Bill Kraft and Joan Huang, and of talking with them, during that particular week at Bellagio, *and* by Du who wrote and Izabel who sang "Bellagio, It's Time to Say Goodbye" at that time also.

Songs of the Wine-Throated Hummingbird

(with thanks to Alexander Skutch's
Life of the Hummingbird)

Down in the sapphire ocean
            the Humpback whales are singing,
maybe about the wonders there,
            how light changes as they descend so that
      their silver day becomes
                  a sable night,
      or about those whippersnapper bottlenoses blowing

great shimmering bubbles then piercing like
spears the silver-quivering
bag of a rising bubble—even as high within
its green radiance of Guatemalan forest
a wine-throated
hummingbird's "sweetly varied outpouring
continues for the better part
of a minute"
—ah, if only
the whales and dolphins swam
in that green light and heard
those tiny singers in their sea of leaves,
such arias they'd interchange,
La Ci Darem La Mano from a great dark whale,
Un Bel Di from high in the frangipani—and then,
imagine the duets,
O Terra Addio at the top
of a dolphin's range, in the center of
a rubythroat's fioriture—
of course
they sing together only
in human words, never I guess in any
but English ones in fact—
in these, if anywhere. Can you hear,
dear reader, how
they sing, you above all who from Africa
brought banjoes and picked up saxophones
then sang the blues all out
of slaveship holds to Harlem, you from every
ocean and continent who understand the songs
of police and ambulance sirens, who record the stars
or white noise from the first Big Bang, is it beyond
imagining how the humpback and
the hummingbird might come out
through parted curtains at the Met for a last
encore? What are sounds,
and what are songs, that we can make them,

that we have ears to hear,
             that on these tiny waves
of air, of water, even of magnetism, we have made
          the smaller ripples that we call Meaning
        when sounds are words—or which, rising
             like Aphrodite from the foam
of dance and song and love, come through as Music? Deep
             in the blue Antarctic seas, high
          in the green Guatemalan jungle, here
          in these cracked English words,
             can you hear them sing,
      the hummingbirds, the humpback whales,
          a neutron star, a human soul?

20

Buck Creek

I wrote that "hummingbird" poem sitting in the Villa Serbelloni, one November day in 1996, a long way in time and space from my Buck Creek days. Yet those days were alive within me, where I sat looking over cypress and olives to the lake, and down at men mowing and trimming and snipping roses or thyme in the tranquil gardens just below my windows there. Watching them made me think of the way my grandfather Aleck Camp used to work around the Buck Creek house and barns and fields.

He had died of a heart attack in March of 1942, and the loss was heavy, not just hard emotionally but also practically, because he was a handy man—the place was falling apart, everything would need fixing, and he was the one who always put things back together, found the baling wire or piece of leather or metal that made things work again. For the last few months of that winter he would take me out with him to milk the cows, and as we walked out to the barn in the cold darkness, me carrying the swinging kerosene lantern, some-thing was different: he might pause to catch his breath, and as we got to the barn and I was herding the Jersey cow in and slipping the rope over her horns and pouring the feed into her pan so she would stand while he milked her, he might be holding a hand over his chest and frowning. He knew the angina was tightening down on him, so he was training me to do the chores before it could take him.

March 1942 was a stormy month—toward the middle, a tor-nado hit the small town of Pryor, over east of us, and wiped out much of it, so we watched the skies and any hanging clouds carefully, all that month. Quite a few days were cold and blustery, others hot and oppressive. On March 25, for the birthday of my twin sister and me, a birthday cake was to be baked, but our mother had come down with a very bad cold or flu, so Grandpa Aleck had baked the cake with her calling directions. It was a two-layer cake, and both layers "fell," so instead of being fluffy and light, the cake was heavy and sirupy under its white soft frosting with that strong vanilla flavor. That was exactly how I liked cake, and we finished off that cake the same day, not a crumb left next morning. And for the weekend, my folks said I could go up and stay over Friday and Saturday nights with my buddy Walter Parks and his family. The Parkses lived a couple of miles to our north, up among the blackjacks on the gravel road to Bowring. So on the Friday after school I rode up there with Walter and his folks, particularly happy because I got to ride in the back next to his sister Janey Belle, with whom I was wildly but secretly in love.

Friday was a warm day, so bright that the tiny buds on the trees seemed to be opening right in front of us. As we headed up the long hill out of our valley, I seem to remember, there was just the faint hint of redbud bloom beginning over at the foot of the hills, behind the thickets of wild plum already putting out white blossoms. When we got to the Parkses' house, their cousin Sammy Fields was there waiting with an invitation to come over, after dinner, to go fishing in their big pond for bass and perch. We ate, then as twilight was falling we went along the rocky rutted dirt road to the pond, and as the moon rose we spread out along the banks and threw out our lines and sat completely quiet, waiting for a bite.

It was a balmy evening, almost warm, no breeze to ruffle the moonlit pond, only the clutter and gronk of bullfrogs around us, until a great horned owl hooted loudly behind us and nearly scared us silly. We looked and saw him sitting on a dead willow stub where he had flown silently up and perched, but he flew off immediately when our voices broke the quiet below. It began to blow then, and turn cooler, and pretty soon we were getting chilly, and it was hard to tell whether our floats were bobbing from a nibble or from the waves. So we gave up fishing and headed back to the Parkses' house.

We had caught a fair mess of fish, which we took back and

cleaned and put away for next day's lunch, but I never got to eat
them, because just after a dawn breakfast the next morning, my
Uncle Bert and brother Antwine came driving into the Parkses' yard
in our blue 1940 Plymouth. Antwine came over and told me we
had to get back home, but he would not say why. I saw Uncle Bert
talking to Walter's dad, and they looked very serious. So I got my
things and climbed in the car's back seat, and Uncle Bert, saying
nothing, started homeward. He drove very fast and did not turn his
head or say anything. I could not figure out what this was all about.
Finally, when Uncle Bert not only came down the long hill without
braking, but floorboarded it once we got to the level county road
toward our meadow and house, I said loudly: "What the hell you
driving so fast for?"

Uncle Bert turned his head sideways, then almost back toward
me, keeping the car straight ahead at sixty miles an hour over that
hissing gravel, and said to me, "Mikey, poor old Grandpa, I'm afraid
he's gone." So we said nothing more till we turned from the road
onto the highway, turned from the highway into our lane, and
pulled up in front of our garage. We got out, went in through the
back door and saw Mom in the kitchen holding my eight-month-old
youngest brother, and the other kids in the dining room as we
passed through, and then we came into the big living room where
Uncle Arthur was standing and Grandpa lay on his back on the bed
at the back of the room. He was fully dressed, and his eyes were
closed, and he looked asleep, with his mouth open. Nobody said
anything, so I walked over and stood beside the bed, and reached
out to push his whiskery jaw up and close his mouth, but it was
rigid and would not close.

Uncle Bert had found him out behind the garage, lying down
near the woodpile from which he had been going to bring in some
wood for the fire to warm the house. The cold front had come
through and it was down in the forties or so. When Grandpa did not
come in with the wood, and Uncle Bert was in the kitchen frying
the bacon and eggs, and could not see him coming back or puttering
around anywhere, he finally moved the big skillet off the fire and
went out to look for him. When he found him, he called my mother
and Antwine and Uncle Arthur to help carry him in. There was no

sign of life at all, and they could not evoke any, so after a while they had remembered somebody must go and bring me back from the Parkses' house.

I was a long time trying to write something for Grandpa. Nothing worked at all well from 1948 through 1956, while I was getting my degrees at Tulsa, at Oxford, and at Yale. Finally when I got my first teaching job at Amherst College, and discovered how to put Oklahoma sounds into the lines (as I mentioned in talking about the Coyote sonnet), I began to find some ways to write about Buck Creek, at first mostly the place and the creatures, the birds and snakes and all. A piece of what emerged in 1957–60 found a place in "Homework at Oxford," which ended up in *An Eagle Nation*. Other pieces, begun during the 1960s, grew and split and coalesced in various ways until about 1968 I put them into "My Right Hand Don't Leave Me No More."

That title is a quotation which I found (so far as I recall) in a newspaper column written by the great Jimmy Cannon, writing about the great Joe Louis. The column must have been written not long before the last fight of Joe Louis, when he came back out of retirement to fight Rocky Marciano. Everybody knew Louis had got too old and slow to fight this young and incredibly tough guy, and the fight went exactly as predicted: Marciano pounded away and Louis finally went down. A day or two before the fight, Jimmy Cannon had written of speaking with Louis as he finished training. Cannon said something like, "How's it going, Joe?" and Louis answered simply, "My right hand don't leave me no more." That seemed to me a revelation. For the first time I thought I could see how it felt to have that kind of quickness, that kind of power: you don't have to "throw" the punch, it just "leaves" you. I have had that kind of feeling only for very minor things, like hitting a return of slam in a Ping-Pong game, where your hand goes out and catches the bullet and hits it back almost before you even "know" that slammed ball is coming at you.

So when I watched the movies of the Marciano–Louis fight, and saw Louis unable to "let it go," to hit Marciano even when Marciano was right in front of him, I remembered seeing the movies of the Louis–Galento fight, some ten years earlier—when Galento, a powerful and fearless mass of muscles, grabbed and fouled and held and pounded Louis for a couple of rounds or so, and knocked him down near the end of a round. Louis bounced up off the floor at once, as if embarrassed and angry, and Galento looked a little surprised and concerned. He looked even more apprehensive at the start of the next round, because it was clear from the whole body-language that Louis was coming after him this round, and for the first time Galento was holding his gloves and watching Louis as if to ward off what was coming. But Galento was one brave bull and he charged in anyhow. Louis had set himself, and you couldn't see the punch, you just saw it land flush on Galento's chin, jarring him staggering back across the ring, almost into the ropes.

That was how Louis had been in the days when he was the man who beat Max Schmeling, and whomever else they put in the ring with him. So he was the man that everybody who had a few drinks would naturally want to be compared with, to the advantage of the man drinking of course. And that was where my grandfather came in, because maybe once in two or three months he would have an extra few drinks and being a man who stood maybe five feet six and weighed a hundred and fifty or so, with each drink his fighting weight went up and by the time he was well into the bottle he was at least two hundred pounds and as he explained to the world he could whip Joe Louis, Jack Dempsey, and John L. Sullivan, maybe all at once. When I was maybe six or seven, I had a few doubts about the truth of these claims, but by the time I was ten or so I had decided that there were better ways of making a fool of yourself than getting drunk and acting like that.

What was hard to believe was that a man who never lied, more sensible and well-behaved and kindly than anybody I knew, could in a saloon or a living room speak total nonsense and solemnly hold it to be self-evident truth. A few years later when I first read that chapter which Mark Twain cut from *Huckleberry Finn*—the one in which the Mississippi raft-men do their drunken boasting—I recognized that this sort of behavior was a way of life in the back-woods, and that my grandfather was doing exactly what his grand-fathers, and all those before him back to the beer-halls of Beowulf, had been doing.

One good thing, though. Loud drunk or quiet sober, Grandpa was good to us kids, never mean, rarely harsh. My mother was in charge of discipline, and generally took an easy line; my Osage step-father Addison would never lift a finger to any of us, and would speak only in the most diffident of ways; so Grandpa was the last resort. He would threaten to use a hickory switch when we were up to no good, but the number of times I recall his using it I can count on the fingers of one hand. My cousin Roy, who lived with us for a couple of years, tells of a time when he was riding Grandpa's saddle horse down to where there were plum trees, and when Roy stood up in the saddle to pick some, suddenly the horse flinched and went sideways. Roy sat back down, then hung on for dear life while the horse went to bucking and then ran frantically up toward the house. Roy yanked on the reins but couldn't stop him, and the horse ran heedless into the barbed-wire fence next to our motor-house. It gashed his leg and side bloody, though it didn't cripple him.

Our grandfather had been out in the yard and saw the horse, with Roy yelling on its back, come storming up through the meadow and run into the fence. Grandpa ran out and stooped through the fence and grabbed the reins and pulled Roy off and gave him a hard swat on his backside with his free hand, then led the horse around to the barn to get some liniment and ointment and doctor it. He said he would be back and take that hickory switch to Roy for doing such a mean and stupid thing. But when Grandpa went to take the saddle off he found a yellowjacket that had got under and stung and stung, and when he came back to the house after the horse was doctored he showed Roy the dead wasp and looked at him and shook his head and said no more, because Roy would know that was his apology for jumping to a wrong conclusion.

So finally, in the early 1960s when we had moved to St. Louis, and I was again able to go back and visit my folks in Buck Creek, I drove through Bartlesville and instead of going directly west and on out to the horseless ranch, I took a two-block detour and drove by what had used to be one of my grandfather's favorite drinking places, the Green Lantern Saloon. It had gone out of business, and being right next to the railway station, it had been converted to the Trailways/Greyhound Bus Depot. Instead of the jaded jollity of the

saloonkeeper, and the edgy defiance of some drinkers, the quiet
despair of others, the noisy bluster of a few down the bar, there
was now the wary glance of the ticket-seller, the mostly weary and
beaten-down manner of the travelers, cheering up suddenly as their
home folks drove up and jumped out of a car to welcome them, or
perking up as the bus pulled in that would trundle them away to
Tulsa or Dallas or Denver or Kansas City.

My Right Hand Don't Leave Me No More

   (Joe Louis to Jimmy Cannon, before the Marciano fight)

When you were drunk, you could always whip Joe Louis—
Lucky he never stopped by Bartlesville
On a Saturday night in the Green Lantern Saloon
Or he'd've been forced to let you knock him out.
I think he'd've done it—not even the local bullies
Would take advantage when you were fighting drunk.
And sober, you were so goddamned meek and truthful
You once outfaced the big fat deputy star
Who came to take our bootlegging uncle away.
Uncle Woody was holding his breath up in the attic—
The sheriff believed he'd been around our place
But thought he'd hid out somewheres back in the hills.
The laws all knew that you never told a lie,
So when they'd searched, this one came out and asked,
"Now Alex, is your boy anywheres around here?"
"Wellsir," you said, straightfaced, "he *was* around."

One time though, I didn't think you'd make it.
Out in the chipstrewn yard beside my window
I saw you face the drunk with his butcher knife.
He raised it over your deprecating hands
And weary eyes, that held its point with meekness.
I saw him halt and scowl, then stumble closer:
"Old man, your time has come. You hear, old man?"
One thing you did kept his knife from slashing—
You did not meet his eyes. I saw him turn

Bewildered eyes to me, and you took the knife
From his passive hands, heard drunken apologies,
Then brought him into the house and had a drink with him.
You dealt with time that way, and better ways.
You fixed the broken farm. It was your hands drove
The shining nail, squeaking under the hammer, into
Its massive gatepost's new-peeled oaken bulk.
I marveled how those huge things yielded to you
Under scrapegong blows of the hammer's bluesteel arc
In the grip of your hands—
I thought your hands that held off shame and poverty
From all of us could keep off death himself,
My grandfather, but I was gone when he came
And did not help. You died bringing in wood for the fire.

21

Losses, One

Sometimes the storms that came through the Buck Creek Valley
were not so apocalyptic as tornadoes, but the lightning they brought
was nothing to take lightly. Years after I had left home and gone to
be a teacher, one of my favorite trees in the old front yard at Buck
Creek was felled by lightning. It was a tall catalpa tree which we
loved to climb, going up as high as we could get almost to the very
top, as dangerous a thing on those brittle limbs as we could have
done. A wonder we did not break our necks or less important bones
many times.

When my brother Jim wrote me that this one, the tallest of the
six catalpas I grew up with, had been struck down, I had to write an
elegy for it. And because our mother had died not so long before the
tree was struck, and this was better than anything I had been able to
write for her, I thought it would be right to give her this one, which
probably was for her all along.

That Lightning's Hard to Climb

For Thelma Louise Camp

—Struck down?
Good Lord, we'd always be
climbing that tall catalpa tree—
its leaves our money, its long bean-pods
cigars, and all of May
we swung and taunted in high

danger and falling blossoms among those great
heart-shaped leaves where a loud beating
of raindrops made us, out on bending
almost-breaking limbs, hunting a taste
of purple-streaked blossoms with gold stamens, feel
sheltered and vulnerable, seeing
how blue sky looked among
sun-lucent leaves as we hung waiting until
bright lines of rain came sweeping
down over us from the leafy hills above
our bluestem meadow and made us
see how the scissortails had placed
their nest beneath a tent of tilting leaves that the wind
kept parting above
their nestlings, and how
the swaying giant held them in its arms as
the flashing giant glanced in
flooding silver down on them and on
their long-tailed mother sitting patient
and streaming off half-opened wings the dancing
spatter, and when
it had gone there was all the twinkle
and diamond flashing in the meadow, the ring and
whistle of robin, of orioles and
redwing blackbird sprinkling again the sunburst
tree in bloom from whose tip
the scissortails towering and inter-
weaving challenges could veer and dip and zoom
up and up, shrieking *treep! tree-eeee-EEP!* building
a musical tree to sing from—
while down below the trunk for us rose solid
from our twilit lawn, a safe base
for wood-tag runners as the dark filled up
with lightning
bugs, stars and cries of
the children running among
the trees while grownups watched from the

gloominous porch, talking of old
and happy faroff things
and laughter long ago—
so now the one
more storm has set blossoms
of fire exploding, now
the Lightning U-Haul has swung down and transported
our half-way house;
                              our swaying path
to the sky whose fall
seems to have saved our house
is gone, and only
some green shoots with their heart-shaped leaves
now mantle where the
living tree once stood.

22

Losses, Two

Our Osage grandmother, Josephine Jump, had died some ten years before our mother did, and it took me several years to find a way to write an elegy for Grandma Jump. Here is what I managed—with some notes that might help understand some of what she meant for us. The Osage words of the epigraph can be translated as "Grandmother, you have come home," with "come home" understood as being the ceremonial phrase for living into the "good days," the time beyond time:

Wazhazhe Grandmother

   —I-ko-eh, tha-gthi a tho.

   Ho-e-ga, literally "bare spot": the center of the forehead of the mythical elk ... a term for an enclosure in which all life takes on bodily form, never to depart therefrom except by death.... the earth which the mythical elk made to be habitable by separating it from the water ... the camp of the tribe when ceremonially pitched ... life as proceeding from the combined influences of the cosmic forces.

   —Francis La Flesche, *A Dictionary of the Osage Language* (1932)

    They chose their allotted land
           out west of the Agency
                  at the prairie's edge,
        where the Osage Hills begin they built
             their homestead, honeymooned there

near Timber Hill,
                    where Bird Creek meanders in
from the rolling grassy plains with their prairie chicken
                              dancing in spring,
          built in a timbered hollow where deer came down
                    at dusk with the stars
                to drink from the deep pools
                    near Timber Hill
                                   and below the
                waterfall that seemed
             so high to me the summer
     when I was six and walked up near its clearness gliding
          some five or six feet down from the flat
             sandstone ledge to its pools;
                         she called it in Osage, *ni-xe,*
          the dark water turning into
                              a spilling of light
                    was a curtain clear and flowing, under
             the blue flash of a kingfisher's diving
             into the pool above the falls

                              and his flying up
          again to the dead white branch of his willow—
             the whole place was so quiet,
                    the way Grandma was quiet,
          it seemed a place to be still,
                    seemed waiting for us,
             though no one lived there by then
          since widowed during the war she'd moved
                to the place south of Pawhuska,
     and why we had driven down there from Timber Hill, now, I
             can't quite remember—
                         was it a picnic, or some kind
          of retreat or vacation time
                out of the August heat of Pawhuska?
                    The pictures focus sharp-edged:

a curtain of dark green ivy ruffled
a bit by breeze and water beside
                the waters falling there
and a dirt road winding red and rocky
                    across tree-roots, along which, carefully,
        my mother eased our rumbling Buick Eight
                in that Depression year when Osage oil
                    still gushed to float us on into
                            a happy future—
but whether I dreamed, or saw real things in time,
            their road, their house, the waterfall back in the woods
                                are all
            at the bottom of Lake Bluestem now,
    because Bird Creek,
                    blessed with a dam,
                            is all Psyched out
    of its snaggly, snaky self into a
                    windsparkling lake
                whose deep blue waters are now
    being piped into Pawhuska pure and drinkable,
                filling with blue brilliance municipal pools
        and sprinkling the lawns to green or pouring freshets
            down asphalt gutters to cool the shimmering
    cicada-droning fevers of August streets
                                even as
    in Bird Creek's old channel under Lake Bluestem,
                            big catfish
        grope slowly in darkness
                up over the sandstone ledge of the drowned
                            waterfall, or
            scavenge through the ooze of
            the homestead and along the road where
an Osage bride and her man came riding one special day
            and climbed down from the buggy in all their
                best finery
                    to live in their first home.

When I was only two my mother had married my fullblood
Osage stepfather Addison Jump, so from my earliest memories our
family was a mix of Osage and "other." The English word *Osage* is
an Anglicized version of the Osage word *Wazhazhe,* so the poem's
title means "Osage Grandmother." It was written for Grandma
Josephine Strikeaxe Jump, who was born in the 1890s, when our
reservation was still in Indian Territory, and who grew up speaking
only Osage. At age ten, a little before the Osage Nation (in 1906)
finally accepted the allotment of tribally held lands to individual
families, she was put into a convent school for four years and learned
to speak English. She must have been still at school when Indian
Territory, in 1907, became part of the new State of Oklahoma.

Not long after that, when she was fourteen, her folks took her
from the school and married her to Jacob Jump. Among the lands
allotted to them was the hundred and sixty acres northwest of
Pawhuska, along Bird Creek and out past Timber Hill, that became
their homestead, where a fine white frame house was built for them.
Their first of four children, my stepfather Addison, was born there
in 1910, followed by my Aunt Arita, Uncle Louis, and their
youngest, Uncle Kenneth, in 1918.

During the years 1910–29, it is said that the Osage Indians
became, per capita, the wealthiest nation in the world: great oil
fields were tapped beneath the Reservation, and among the still
flourishing oil companies founded on that strike are Phillips 66 and
Conoco. (Frank Phillips was made an honorary Osage.) Maybe the
best account of those years is given in a 1934 novel called *Sundown,*
written by an Osage scholar and savant named John Joseph
Mathews (it's still in paperback, now from the University of
Oklahoma Press), whose father served on the Osage Tribal Council
during the insane orgies of spending and exploitation of the period
between 1907 and 1929. The Mathews family were mixed-bloods
descended from the marriage of an Osage woman and a preacher
and mountain man named Old Bill Williams, for whom eventually a
river in Arizona was named.

John Joseph Mathews himself went to the University of
Oklahoma, became a flyer during World War One, won a Rhodes

Scholarship to Oxford but used his own money to go to Merton
College and take a degree, then head over to the boulevards of
Paris and the streets of Geneva where he covered the founding of
the League of Nations. Mathews had all the money he wanted but
was too restless to stay in Paris with the likes of Fitzgerald and
Hemingway, so he took his motorcycle down to Morocco and rode
around there for a while, but seeing once some splendid horsemen
charging across the country firing their rifles thought them so like
the Osages and the cowboys back on the reservation that he got
homesick, so he came back. Before he settled again in Pawhuska, the
Osage Agency town, he did some time in Los Angeles in the late
twenties selling real estate, getting married, and partying.

Only after the Depression hit did he come back to Pawhuska,
build him a rock house out in the prairie-and-blackjack-oaks north
of Pawhuska, and begin to do scholarly work, first producing a Book
of the Month Club winner called *Wahkontah: The Osage and the
White Man's Road* (based on the diaries and memoirs of a nineteenth-
century agent to the Osages, an uncle I think of Herbert Hoover) for
the newly founded Oklahoma University Press, where a younger
Rhodes scholar named Joseph Brandt was looking for good writers.
Mathews served on the Osage Tribal Council for three terms,
founded the Osage Tribal Museum, and wrote a splendid history of
the Osages.

But Jacob Jump, my stepfather's father, was a soldier during
World War One, and he died in the great influenza epidemic after
it ended. Grandma Jump and the children then lived a good deal
with Jacob's mother, who herself had been widowed and had
remarried one of the wealthiest of the Osages, Pierce St. John, and
they had three more children, two uncles and an aunt of my stepfather Addison. Pierce St. John had a great deal of land south of
Pawhuska, and he left my grandmother Josephine eighty acres down
there, on which she and my stepfather and her other children lived
from the early 1920s. They had a fine small house there, along with
another house that they rented to the tenant farmers who managed
their farm. When Addison married my mother in 1933, we first
lived in Pawhuska, in a rented house on Big Hill, over behind the

Osage Agency buildings and grounds—not far from the Million
Dollar Oak under which the oil-lease auctions were held.

I have some early memories of that Pawhuska house, but in
the spring of 1934 when I was three we moved to a house twenty
miles east, in the Buck Creek Valley, and I grew up and lived twenty
years in the Buck Creek community, going to school in a one-room
country school of eight grades, numbering usually between twenty
and forty students taught by a single teacher. Our house was on
eighty acres, mostly bluestem hay but with some wheat and corn
land. We used to go over and visit Grandma Josephine and Uncle
Kenneth and Aunt Arita south of Pawhuska, but once in a while we
might also go down to visit the old homestead west and north of
Pawhuska, on Bird Creek, where Grandma Josephine and Jacob
Jump had first lived, and where I think they stayed now and then if
some kind of work was being done on the house south of Pawhuska.

Grandma Josephine lived to be well over seventy. All her life
she spoke English with a strong Osage accent, and she and her friends
all spoke Osage to each other most of the time. I have a tape record-
ing made in 1965 in which Grandma and Julia Whitehorn (née
Lookout) are talking in Osage of the good old days, and Grandma
slowly and gently tells of the occasion in September 1952 when a
Naming Ceremony was held for me and my Osage name was given
me. I used to play the tape for my classes in American Indian
Literature, partly because when she tells the story she goes on to say
that after I had gone over to study in England I came back to the
United States to teach and that I was now living in St. Louis. The
students in my classes would be listening along to her slow careful
telling in Osage of this story, and then suddenly in the midst of the
Osage words they could hear her pause and say, ever so carefully,
Saint Louis.

So when she died in the early 1970s I kept wanting to write
something for her, but not until about 1974 or 1975 did a way of
doing this come to me. That was when I went back to Pawhuska to
visit Aunt Arita, who by then had sold the old house south of
Pawhuska and moved in to live on Revard Avenue in Pawhuska. I
knew that the family had long ago had to sell the old homestead
place by Timber Hill on Bird Creek, but this time I heard that at

last the long-rumored dam was being built on Bird Creek for a city water supply, and that the lake would cover the old homestead. Now, I thought, one more Indian home is going under water. So I wrote the poem, and when a new publication at the University of Arizona called *Sun Tracks* asked me if I had any poems for its editors to consider, I sent "Wazhazhe Grandmother" along, and it came out there in 1976.

23

Losses, Three

I've mentioned that my Irish and Scotch-Irish grandfather, James Alexander Camp, died in 1942. He was born February 28, 1870, in the Big Thicket country of northeast Texas, not so far south of the Red River and Indian Territory (as Oklahoma then was)—six years before Custer got his, and two years after Custer had massacred the Cheyenne village of Black Kettle on the Washita River in that territory. As a child of some three years old, he had wandered away from his home into the woods and was lost for three days and nights.

A year or so later, his family moved north to Missouri, settling near Doniphan in Ripley County, a few miles north of the Arkansas line, on a farm near the Current River. He grew up there, married in the late 1890s a woman who was also Irish, and from 1898 to 1914 they had seven children—my mother and her six brothers. When his wife Margaret died of breast cancer—not so long after their last child, my Uncle Woody, was born—Grandpa Camp took the children and went out to the wheat harvest in Kansas one summer in a covered wagon. They worked also, my grandfather and the oldest boys, in the lead and zinc mines around Picher, Oklahoma.

Hearing of the great oil boom and the need for teams and men to help build the boom towns of the Osage Reservation, where gushers were coming in every day, they got in the covered wagon and headed southwest to the Agency town of Pawhuska. There, with the mules Old Beck and Jude, Grandpa and the boys hauled bricks and timber, and helped put up the buildings in Pawhuska, from about 1916 onward. My mother and her brother Woody went to the

Pawhuska schools, the older boys having dropped out of school
after a few grades and mostly, when not helling around somewhere,
helping with the work. Grandpa made good wages for several years
and bought a house in Pawhuska, but it turned out the real estate
people knew the new railroad would be coming through just where
they sold him a place, so he lost the house—just when the postwar
depression years hit in 1921–22 or so, and he couldn't buy another
one. The boys started running wild, with plenty of white lightning
to fuel things after Prohibition began in 1919. Oklahoma had always
been officially dry, so Prohibition just added a layer of Federal police
to stomp people harder.

My grandfather was sixty-four by the time my mother had
married my stepfather Addison, and they bought the eighty acres of
Osage-allotment land from another Osage family that had gone
bankrupt in the Depression (the oil money quit just then), with its
house and barns and motor-house and chickenhouse and two-car
garage in Buck Creek. So Grandpa gave up his by-then moribund
hauling and contracting in Pawhuska, and came out to Buck Creek
to help run the farm. For maybe four years, while there was enough
Osage oil money still in reserve to cover expenses and try to raise a
few crops and run some cattle, things went pretty well, but once the
money trickled out and the Dust Bowl times were on us, nothing
could keep a small farm afloat, and we sank into really hard times,
getting by on the pittance of Osage oil money still coming in to my
stepfather, and whatever day labor he could find.

It helped when (in 1940) the tiny Social Security pension
began to be paid to Grandpa, and we boys and any resident uncles
(they came and stayed a while between engagements, now and then)
worked for small pay at hoeing corn, shocking wheat, baling and
hauling hay. For his last four years or so, until he died on March 28,
1942, my grandfather could see things were really going to be tough
for this family for some time, and it must have been pretty discour-
aging for him to see things go downhill there in Buck Creek.

When we moved in, the place had its own electricity generator
—so electric lights lit the house, and the "motor house" had a pump
that brought, from a well, water for indoor plumbing: toilet, bath,
kitchen sink. But by 1939 the pump-motor died, and so did the

generator. We studied by kerosene lamps, and took baths in wash-tubs of water heated on the kitchen stove, and did laundry in water hand-drawn from the well or cistern and heated in great oil-drums over outdoor fires. Then too, we had to dig a privy-pit and set an outhouse over it, and for several years we used that outdoor one-hole privy, not the warmest of places on a winter's day, nor the most fragrant on a hot summer day. Grandpa was a handy man with tools, and along with my older brother Antwine and our stepfather did what seemed possible.

About 1941, when Grandpa was over seventy, the privy-hole was full and we had to dig a new pit, fill in the old one, and move the outhouse over to the new pit. Years after my grandfather died, in 1968, I finally wrote an elegy for him, "My Right Hand Don't Leave Me No More." But a few years later there came back to me the comic moment when we were moving the outhouse off the old pit so we could put it over the new one, and I saw that this was a time when what happened to him, and how he managed it, showed the kind of man he was pretty well. So I wrote this other poem for him.

Pure Country

I.

Pick and shovel dug the privy-hole square
    down into orange clay
under the garden's loam,
        a foot of black soil,
    two feet of pebbly grayness,
then clay and the pale harsh rocks
    in shovelfuls grating up
    to splat on the loose-sided mound
next to the pit,
        then shoveling the mound out over
    the garden soil around it
and shoving, levering the white clapboard privy
    on rollers until it was perched above

the eight-foot pit
on steel pipes,
plunking the loam
and clay around its bottom edges firm,
going in, stamping, rocking, leveling, and seeing
that the door would swing
open, and close, and the hook to latch it
worked just fine.

2.

The water-well pierced down and down through loam,
through clay, through pebbles and
bedrock by pick and sledges and
spike and shovel, buckets on
ropes to take the dirt up
then setting flat rocks atop each other round
and around its roundness when the water began
to rise and fill and darken; rocking in
the sides completely, sanding
the bottom over,
how deep? twenty feet
to the splash, twelve feet that the bucket
would sink on down slowly, pause
and settle, until a pull
would bring it dreaming upward so it broke
the darklit surface with a Floosh!
and like a soul in flesh grew heavy
but rose to the straining hands
full of light-sparkles shaking
and fresh rock-tasting water spilling
back down the dark echoes to where
it shivered alive with breathing.

3.

In the privy after five years or so
bluegreen bottle-flies humming

around the toilet-hole, the loose newspapers
brown-stained and musty with the news
of last year's football, wars
and sermon topics, down in
the acrid darkness webs sticky
in masses, sparkling here and there
bluegreenly with the shells
of flies sucked dry and the oily
gleam of black widows waiting
below and to the side of
the naked bottoms there on the hole above them,
flies drawn by the smell,
spiders after the flies,
filth rising to meet them.

4.

The year we moved the privy
from its old pit filled and stinking
to the new and fresh-dug one,
we shoveled earth into and over
the old one and stamped it quaking down,
but it did not let us off
untouched, the oldest of us missed
his footing when a pipe gave way and he slowly sank
up to his chest in the liquid stuff
before he could grab a rope,
and we pulled our grandfather up
with a heave, looked at each other's faces and
broke out laughing like hell and he—
without a single word even to swear, he looked
down at his dripping self for a minute and then
turned and walked silent along
the path to the well
                    stripping his clothes as he walked,
and at the well drew up the buckets full
of sun-bright water and moving away

poured it all over him, scrubbed
and poured and then soaped and poured and
scrubbed and poured
till he was clean in
the dry September day and walked
in the house and got clean clothes and came out
and we moved the privy on out
above its new-dug hole.

24

Leaving Tracks
Ponca, Osage, and Others

One June, our son Lawrence and I drove down to visit our Ponca
relatives Mike and Casey and their children, who were then living
near Fairfax on the Osage Reservation. We stayed in their house up
on a hilltop among trees, and that night there was a huge thunderstorm, spectacular lightning and thunder, wind and drenching rain
swirling and moving in rain-ghosts among the flashes. Much better
than television, whose electrons rarely persuade us (as lightning's
do) that any minute now the Sweet Chariot may be Swinging Low:
those cop-show car-chases are only fiction, whereas a lightning-split
oak tree, and the roaring of Salt Creek rising, are not "made in
Hollywood."

It's the next day I'm talking about, though—when we walked
out of the house, surprisingly unshattered, into a rare blue-brilliant
day. We followed a back way down toward Salt Creek to see how
things stood, if they still stood. And as we walked along a part of
the path that was level and had not been gullied, we skirted a clear
shallow puddle in whose silty bottom there were still tracks of a
possum, under a half-inch of still water. As I followed Lawrence and
Wesley (Mi-ka-si), I saw they were leaving tracks right alongside
those of last night's possum, and I noticed off to the side, in the tall
bluestem, some brilliant orange "butterfly weed" with a tiger swallowtail on them, a huge gold and black-striped being with rainbow

spots, saw it lift up from those orange flowers and float over to some blue morning glories draping a bank. So later I got to thinking about these things, and I thought I would try to put something into words that might get across to our children when we have gone ahead far enough that this would be our best chance of being heard:

Over by Fairfax, Leaving Tracks

The storm's track is
a fresh blue sky over
Salt Creek running brown
and quick, and a huge tiger
swallowtail tasting the brilliant
orange flowers beside our trail.
Lightning and thunder've spread
a clean sheet of water over
these last-night possum tracks
straight-walking like a dinosaur in
the mud, and next to these we've
left stippled tracks from soles made
in Hong Kong, maybe with Osage oil.
Lawrence and Wesley pick blue-speckled flints
along our path, one Ponca boy
in braids, one Osage son
in cowboy hat.
Over the blue Pacific, green Atlantic we
have come together here—possum's
the oldest furred being in this New World, we
are newest in his Old World.
Far older, though—
but younger too—the tiger swallowtail
goes sailing from her orange milkweed to
some sky-blue nectar: the wild morning
glories will spring up
where she's touched down, marking
her NEXT year's trail.

Makes me wonder—
if archaeologists should ever dig our prints
with Possum's here, whether they'll see
the winged beings who moved
in brightness near us, leaving no tracks except
in flowers and
these winged words.

25

Going to College

Well, so ... language is winged words, is getting across, is leaving tracks. Wordsmiths do funny things to time and space. That can be illustrated in all kinds of ways, and in 1990 I got to thinking about how a television program does such peculiar things to time and space and human awareness. The University of Tulsa honored me, that May, with a kind of retroactive Phi Beta Kappa key—when I was an undergraduate, T.U. had no Phi Beta Kappa chapter, only a local honorary, with the same kind of standards but without the national cachet.

One price I'd have to pay for the key would be to think of something to say that would not show everybody how far short of Phi Bete I was. A lot of my audience would be Petroleum Engineers, for instance, and it seemed a good idea not to show complete ignorance of the contributions by engineers to our society. I got to thinking about the marvels of time and space with which engineers have let us play in a TV set. That was just while I was watching a TV program called *The Living World*, and this gave me an idea for a poem to read at the Phi Beta Kappa ceremony coming up in Tulsa. Reading a fairly short poem, I thought, might spare both me and the audience—spare me the pains of composing a lecture, and spare them the boredom of hearing it. If they hated poems, or were bored by this one, at least it would be brief.

But of course I had to lead up to the poem, so I ended by composing a kind of talk anyhow. Composing it, I kept in mind that machines and mathematical symbols transform time and space at least as powerfully as do the words of a natural language like English or Osage. I had been thinking anyhow of petroleum engineers, drilling tens of thousands of feet below the dawn in Oklahoma or Montana to bring our kitchens hot turquoise flowers of fossil sunlight to perk our breakfast coffee, bubbling there on the everyday miracle of a gas stove. I thought, too, of crazy astrophysicists, playing with some pure and useless kind of math that ends up expanding the universe, or explaining black holes, or making computers more friendly. It still amazes me that you can take an apple, a galaxy, and a cobra and just "class" them as "numbers"—ONE, TWO, THREE—as if the differences mattered not at all, as if all beings were entirely and supernaturally and democratically equivalent in the ghost-world of numbers. An engineer must completely ghost-dance the world before transforming it, since the numbers which re-present its beings, "re-presence" them, must pretend not to know the limits of apple pollen, or cobra genes, or light-years.

More stupefying still to think of the engineers who "discovered" that whirling copper wires around a magnet will generate electric current: Michael Faraday and others who took the lodestone, that little toy of Greek and Roman children, a stone rejected by any sensible builders, and made it the cornerstone of our civilization. Surely THAT magic is as interesting as language, and surely the miles of copper wire or quartz tubules or bodiless laser-beams, the waves of messages pulsing through space from Moscow to Miami, from Tulsa to Timbuctoo, are bridges as dangerous and safe as the one over Buck Creek in Osage country.

The bridges work, of course, only when they have been mapped into numbers, translated into ohms and watts and amperes—all the proper nouns, these personal names of long-dead men who arranged for the drowned rainbows of the Grand Canyon, whose ghosts now haunt the depths of Lake Mead and Glen Canyon, to flash up through the wires and emerge as a brilliant Phoenix in Arizona, or a neon Bird of Paradise in Las Vegas.

Nor is it enough for the engineers to turn natural rainbows into civilized neon. Think how they have caged us all within the wired walls of our homes, surrounded like canaries by all that copper wiring. Think of us in these electric cages, tingling with thunderbolts from all those great fat lakes, those blazing coal furnaces, those freeze-framed nuclear explosions: think how at every wall-socket the thunder's power awaits our touch, thanks to the Engineers and the Mathematics majors.

And Thunder is not cast in minor roles by these composers. Like the Osage elders, who still speak to us from the great volumes of the Bureau of American Ethnology on the back shelves of our library crypts, the Engineers have met the Thunder Being and accepted his gracious offer. To the Osages, and to the Engineers, Thunder has said: *If you make your bodies of me, you will live to see old age, and live into the happy days.* That was what was said to Osages when they decided to come down from the stars and become a nation on this earth. (Being sensible people, the Osages had sent scouts ahead to find out what it might be like, this new world, and their scouts met many beings who were gracious in offering to give their bodies and show them how to live successfully in this world: Black Bear, Deer, Golden Eagle, Cedar Tree, Mountain Lion, Thunder.)

I think that just as Thunder offered himself to the Osages, so also to the Europeans—to Michael Faraday, James Clerk Maxwell, Albert Einstein, Claude Shannon. When I was given an Osage name to carry, it was as one member of the Thunder clan: the name I was given had been spoken by the first Osages to meet Thunder as they were coming down from the stars to live on this world. Meeting Thunder, they were struck with fear, but he greeted them graciously and gave them his powers, saying: "If you make your bodies of me, you will live to see old age, and live into the peaceful days." That was one way Osages got across from stars to earth, from being a huddled mass of humanity to being a nation.

It seems to me the Osage people have used Thunder's powers reasonably well—certainly the part of this continent they lived in, when the Europeans reached it, was still a place of great plenty, of drinkable streams, of edible plants and animals, of everything humans need and want. No child of Europe, coming by hook or crook into such an inheritance, could complain of being short-changed.

Maybe the Europeans have not always used the Thunder's powers quite so responsibly, though more extensively. Hiroshima,

Nagasaki, Chernobyl have shortened a few lives. But that is only part of the story: think how the engineers have encouraged electrons to change their ways, how eagerly particles of possibility wait to leap from our wall-sockets—electrons, just waves or condensations in space, much like words in the air—and how cleverly the Engineers have tamed these tigers, how many platforms they have trained them to leap upon and perform amazing tricks. They flash into a radio and come out as Caruso, the long-dead Caruso, alive and gloriously singing once more. Or they charge into a TV, hit the glowing screen in perfect formation, and produce ... well, oddly enough, at times they produce something on TV called *The Living World,* which once produced in me, or in an electronic word-processor where my fingers played for a time, a sequence of words, which I have called "Sea-Changes."

This is a poem about getting across, and language, and electronic and mathematical transformations—here, the languages of humans and dolphins. Although it swam into these words from a long time back in my life, and even though when I was writing it I thought only of trying to get certain things said that mattered a lot, yet even when it was being coaxed into and out of its own electrons, I could see it might fit that Phi Beta Kappa occasion—because it IS about getting across time and space, and how aliens might hear each other, if they could. At its end, both alien speaker and alien listener are sometimes human beings—a good thing to remember, five hundred years after Indians discovered Columbus playing around on their beaches with dangerous instruments.

Sea-Changes, Easter 1990

—Poem for Phi Beta Kappas, University of Tulsa, 4 May 1990

For Don and Mary Frances Hayden

Where the electron gun targets the screen
between the past and us, we push
the buttons that will resurrect
The Living World within our living room, so we
can watch dolphin and diver try

to comprehend each other's mind,
The mind, that ocean where each kind
Does straight its own resemblance find;
Yet it creates, transcending these,
Far other worlds, and other seas:
we sink down where
the pale blue quivers as a dolphin swims
out of her dark shadows into
our hearts and minds. I think she hears, mostly,
a plume of silver bubbles rising from
this clumsy alien and the buzzing box he holds,
some glass-eyed thing that never, so far
as the dolphin knows, looks back at her—
yet here, from deep behind its glass
in this *dark forward and abysm of time,*
we sit looking into that dolphin's eyes and wonder
what goes on deep within her where
a consciousness of self and us might be. And words
come bubbling from our television, spoken
months later and thousands of miles away from where
diver and dolphin face each other, saying:
"We tried to speak with dolphins—knowing
they have a kind of language, we were hoping
to send a message."
—Now the diver has carried down into
the dreaming turquoise of
the dolphin's parlor ordinary jars:
they might be fruit-juice jars but in this medium they
morph into sun-seines, crystal star-traps—and now
the diver takes his air-tube from his mouth,
inverts a jar and jams the tube up into
its mouth so silver bubbles fill
it with brilliant air and then
he does it to other jars, two, THREE of them,
and see, he's got a little rod to tap them with—
he's tapping, and we hear each jar
respond with different tone, he makes almost

a tune—it is enchanting, and look—from shadows there
offstage the dolphin eases toward the jars, she noses
up past them, eyeing
the diver and his jars, she clearly
listens, and looks, and wonders maybe . . . ah no,
she turns, and her tail waves like a conductor damping down
to pianissimo, she swims away into
the darkness, saying with her whole body:
They'll NEVER speak: they have no music!
Disappointed, the diver
descends now to the white fine sand
of the seabottom and glances towards the anchor-chain
of the boat he's dived from, trailing there. He reaches down,
he picks it up, he looks: we see
the chainlinks glitter, hear the clinks
and scrapes, we see the anchor's flukes
unfold, as he lifts it, in his weightless dreamlit
heaven of Zuni silversmiths where he has set
the turquoise tingling with his silver anchorchain—
and SWIFTLY NOW from where
the blue turns black, a shape comes hurtling, but
she turns and slows, she passes over the jangling
silver chain, she looks,
listens, poises
quite upside down and drifts, beak slightly open, listens to
those tinny squeaks, clinks, scrapings, clanks: her eyes
lost in ecstatic hearing, her head as close
to the chain as she can get, saying:
At last, a Tristan for my Isolde! how could they ever
encrypt this miracle of music in such links of light, who
could ever have composed it and was he the greatest lover of all
the dolphins in the world?
Well, OF COURSE!
We always knew the messages we sent
with Voyager would get across, though what
we didn't know was what those messages might mean:
the Navajo Night Chant, maybe THAT would heal

the wars out there? or would it take
the sound of crickets, or the clink
of chains in medieval dungeons? Perhaps the rasping
of dull razorblades across
a three-day stubble, or the screek
of chalk on blackboards, THAT
will be Beethoven—
our long-dead Star rising to shine within
their WAVE OF FAME? *Humans,*
they'll maybe say,
they can't be ALL bad, if they can sing like that!
But there's a DOWN side, though—
could be, Beethoven's Ninth
and its great Ode to Joy
will translate as a declaration of merciless
War upon the beings of the first
palm-fringed star where Voyager
has washed up with our brittle jetsam.
—What DID the Aztecs hear, when the white sails
of Cortez rose from a turquoise sea?
Five hundred years ago, we've heard,
five hundred years ago Columbus came:
what messages our people then exchanged, what chains
of promises we heard. AND buffaloes, passenger pigeons,
Pequods and Mohicans heard: "we" sent "them"
tomatoes and syphilis, "they" gave "us"
the Civil Wars of aliens. So now we peer
into the eyes of natives trapped in the ruined walls
of Dresden, Hue, Beirut, El Salvador—

EL SALVADOR!

paralyzed children staring
into the Pulitzer Prizes of our televising selves,
on Easter Sunday like flying fish we skim
the rainbow waves of
a Religious Channel purpled by the death

and resurrection of that Savior
whom Michaelangelo sculpted for his Pope—
breakfasting at home,
we look down from within the dome
of St. Peter's there in Rome:
what music's there, what anchorchains
of hope, what alien sounds
we roll away the tombstones from, what alien eyes
we look into and try to comprehend.

I don't know that this poem ends on a note of optimism about how we can get across the distances of which I have been speaking. The screen between us and the past is, after all, more than the glass of a television tube.

But we should remember that a small group of persons who have shown themselves unusually able to learn from the regular curriculum what their teachers want them to learn—new Phi Beta Kappas, for instance—are supposed to include the bridge-builders, the language-translators, the power-transformers who will help us get across time and space and the rivers of Babylon to significant others, even as we are swinging dangerously into the future. Such people may help resurrect the living world in our television set, our box of far-seeing (to zap that Greek and Latin word television into English, make it mintier on our tongues maybe). They number for us the streets of chaos, play the music a dolphin wants to hear—if the right words, the right equations, the right thunder beings come help us hear and understand.

And here is where I can bring this off-track chariot of words full circle, back to the time when I first arrived at Tulsa University, having voyaged in my seventeen-year-old innocence across the great distance between Buck Creek Rural Community on the Osage Reservation, and the monstrous alien metropolis of Tulsa with its unknown, unknowable University. Common sense would know I was bound to fail, could never get across that distance. We know that children born into poverty, whose parents and folks all "lack education and social skills," particularly any child with one uncle killed hijacking bootleg whisky shipments while out on parole from robbing a bank, another uncle beaten to death by police in the local jail, all such children in raggedy clothes apt to hide in shame when strangers come to the door, must be doomed to a life of misery, failure, crime, underachievement.

Sure, we *know* this. I should stipulate at once, however, that if you really do know any people like us, my folks and me, you've noticed that they're as smart as rich people, probably less selfish on the average, just as funny and decent—or, I suspect, more so—and you know they are on the average a good kind of people to grow up with. If you yourself grew up among well-to-do folks with rugs on the floor, writing checks that didn't bounce, among adolescents in prep schools who might occasionally wonder why other pimple-poppers their age aren't getting Porsches for graduation—then you may not ever attain a status, among my kind of people, other than alien. You may find it too hard to learn that the difference between poor and rich people is that the poor don't know as much about making money or keeping it, and mostly don't care as deeply about it, a weakness that may be genetic (surely there is as likely to be a gene for acquisitiveness, for Scrooging, as one for intelligence, for Einsteining?).

Well, there *are* other differences perhaps. It is harder for poor people to find others to look down on. It is harder for them to get good medical treatment, or be looked at without suspicion and resentment when they seek it.

But here I am only telling how I got across Buck Creek to Oxford. My path went through the University of Tulsa, which raises the question: what WAS the University of Tulsa? At that time, it did not have a Phi Beta Kappa chapter, it was nearly bankrupt, did not have a faculty of mostly Ph.D.'s, nor a library containing all the commentaries on commentaries, and criticisms of criticisms, which university libraries now must have to be certified and respectable. I don't know what I would have done at Harvard University, or any place that considered itself good enough to look down on some country kid with fifty dollars to his name and no idea how to put a nickel into a pay phone and dial a number—which was my problem when looking for a job that might let me eat while going to college, a problem caused by the fact that I grew up in a house

without electricity or telephones, and on the few occasions when I
used a phone there were operators who worked its magic for me.

But whatever Tulsa University was not—had not—did not,
what it WAS for me was Franklin Eikenberry, Don Hayden, Paul
Alworth, Mary Clay Williams, and some other wonderful teachers,
administrators, and friends, not to speak of some extremely bright
students I could name—Bob Stevick, Liz Neely, George Everett,
Bonnie Bledsoe, Bob Taylor, Harriet Lester, Ken Rucinski, Laura
Hume, Betty Davis, Bill Winchester, Paul Dykes, and others. And
when I talk of teachers, I don't mean they were just GOOD guys. I
once unintentionally (I think!) insulted an Oxford University tutor
I respected, Hugo Dyson—one of the Inklings, friend of Tolkien
and of C. S. Lewis, and my literary tutor at Merton College—by
telling him I thought his Shakespeare lectures were very good,
ALMOST as good as those of Professor Eikenberry at the
University of Tulsa.

It was not an idle compliment. On a good day, Mr. Eikenberry—
who never got his Ph.D., his graduate work having been cut down
by the Depression—was the best lecturer I ever heard.[5] True, his
lectures were as much wilderness as garden. There were lots of
tangled thorny throat-clearings, much desperate clinking of keys in
pockets, while he waited for the Muse of Shakespearean Commentary to descend, or to take flight like a swallow—but descend she
did sometimes, and flew as gracefully as swallows, and we had a
wilderness fuller than Eden of fruitful insights, where fresh names
and phrases touched the amazing beings of Shakespeare's plays. I
felt sometimes like Adam waking up and finding what was in this
world he had been given. I took my freshman English Composition
with him, and one of the poems he had us discuss was Shakespeare's
Sonnet 29:

When, in disgrace with fortune and men's eyes,
I all alone beweep my outcast state,
And trouble deaf heaven with my bootless cries,
And look upon myself and curse my fate,
Wishing me like to one more rich in hope,
Featured like him, like him with friends possessed,

Desiring this man's art, and that man's scope,
With what I most enjoy contented least—
Yet in these thoughts myself almost despising,
Haply I think on thee: and then my state,
Like to the lark at break of day arising
From sullen earth, sings hymns at heaven's gate—
For thy sweet love remembered such wealth brings
That then I scorn to change my state with kings.

When I try to recall the actual words Professor Eikenberry
used as he talked with us about this poem, it seems to me we
crossed BENEATH the bridge—not journeying as usual over the
surface words and lines. He took us into the scary place Shakespeare
describes, let us know what those words were talking about, that
homeless sewer of self-doubt, and showed us how astonishing and
healing it was to see that one of the greatest poets ever to write in
English could value himself so little, and envy others so much. But
as Mr. Eikenberry said, this is not just a poem about being down, it
is a poem about getting back up after being down, it is a friendship
poem and a love poem, it tells us that getting across to another
human being is a better cure for what ails us than being a wealthy
monarch.

And one surprising thing that helped me, reading this poem for
his classes, was that I grew up in the country, in a house surrounded
by eighty acres of tall bluestem where the meadowlarks nested. If
Shakespeare wanted to tell me that to remember suddenly the love
of a really good friend is like a lark flying up and singing as it flies,
I was ready to hear that comparison, I had spent a lot of mornings
going out in the early dawn, before the sun had come through the
horizon and turned its dew to diamonds, when there were still no
shadows and the meadowlarks were fluttering and singing, singing
and flying, in the watered and shadowless light.

I understood that these were not Shakespeare's skylarks, that it
was not all the way up to heaven's gate that our meadowlarks flew,
but across an Oklahoma meadow, where the bobwhites perched on
fenceposts and showed me a steadier way to state your family values.
But what Professor Eikenberry did was to show us that no matter

how lovely the images, how gorgeous the sound, how brilliant the structure and language, *these sonnets were about shared experience, not alien mysteries.*

So when I went to the wheat harvest, the summer after that freshman year, trying to earn enough money for another year at the university, I carried in my suitcase—which got pretty heavy as a result—the copy of Shakespeare's works that Professor Eikenberry, seeing I had no money to buy it, gave me from his own shelves. And we wrote back and forth about those plays and sonnets, and when I came to the middle of August and realized I had not saved up enough to manage the tuition and living expenses and would have to get a job or go into the Army, I wrote to Professor Eikenberry to say so.

What he did was to telephone me, where I was staying up in Kansas, in the farmhouse of Calvin and Mary Ellen Parker near the hamlet of Palco and the town of Plainville. He told me not to let go, to hang on a little longer, because there was a new scholarship that had just been endowed by H. O. McClure and I was eligible and he was going to put my name in for it.

The next time he telephoned, a few days later, he told me I was being offered a McClure Scholarship. I said I was not sure, even with the tuition plus that it paid, that I could manage. He said not only could I be assured of a hundred hours of work a month (at fifty cents an hour, that would cover my basic rent and food), but he would see to it that any shortfall would be taken care of. He was offering to help me out of his own pocket, though he had no money but a very small professor's salary to live on. And he did, and while I tried to repay him when I later was earning money on my own, there is no way such befriending can be repaid, except by trying when possible to do the same for someone else, and to some extent by remembering and by these words.

But when I got off the telephone that day in Kansas, and went out to tell my buddy Walter Parks and his sister Mary Ellen and her husband Calvin, and there were meadowlarks singing out in the fields, I had no doubt at all what Shakespeare meant by comparing his change of state to the song and flight of a skylark, and linking it to the remembrance of a really good friend.

So that is one way to tell you what the University of Tulsa was, fifty years ago. But there was more. I mentioned Don Hayden, and I could praise his teaching all right, because it was terrific. I first studied Chaucer with him, and when I got to Oxford I stood in there with those Brits, bright as they were, and was able to read the Middle English aloud as well as they did, though I'll never write an essay with such lucid elegance as they all seemed able to manage. Maybe the fact that a major focus of my scholarly work is medieval English literature will suggest that Don Hayden did his work well in the Chaucer class. But his Shelley and Keats course was even more full of astonishing ideas and history, alive with current debate and theory, and his seminar on Romanticism was as packed and challenging a course as I have had anywhere, Oxford or Yale or wherever.

Still, that was just the classroom side. I have to tell you that on the first day I got to the university and went to the English Department to get enrolled, I had not yet found a room and did not know how to find one. So I asked them what I could do. What Professor Eikenberry did was turn me over to Don Hayden, then a recent Ph.D. from Syracuse and a new assistant professor at Tulsa, teaching four courses and handling a host of other duties. Don Hayden put me into his car, drove me around Tulsa to several places to choose one in which I could stay, quietly made sure it was not people who would cheat or scant me, but good people (the Hughes family on South Gary) in whose house I would be staying, and *then* he brought me back to campus. He did this like an English gentleman: as if it were simple, natural, and no trouble. I did not then know, though I soon found out when I became a student assistant in the department, how hectic a time enrollment week was for teachers with chores of all sorts, heavy teaching loads, family responsibilities, everything that tries to keep them chained to office and classroom and hallway.

The poem I have talked about already, "Getting Across," tells how a boy tries to cross a creek by swinging, hand over hand, along the girders beneath the bridge, and at last has to get up onto the ledge on the other side. It tells that when he kicked up his leg and put his foot onto that ledge, the others reached out and pulled him to its safety, for the time being. I remember this, when I think of what the University of Tulsa and its teachers were, before the safe highways, the solid libraries, the strong curricula, the Ivy League faculty, had made it a much more prestigious place to hang out.

I wouldn't counsel anyone to cross every bridge in so clumsy, dangerous, and quirky a way as the poem pictures. Yet people will cross, somehow or other—when that bridge was out, we'd climb down and wade, or sometimes swim—but most of my life I've been glad to drive a safe car over routine bridges. I try nevertheless to remember that where now deep water winks as we zoom over a bridge, once others crossed only with difficulty; where there now are guides, mentors, Phi Beta Kappa chapters to make straight the way, a long time ago someone planned, arranged for, paid for, put in place these bridges. It is worth remembering how much it takes to build bridges, if we ever can, over the dangerous and impassable distances within and between us. And maybe it is worth saying, to anyone who may be crossers of these gulfs, bridgers of these distances, that I hope in time you will be kind to an alien, and show that you are not only Phi Beta Kappas, but good human beings. ONE day an alien may have a chance to thank you for it.

Irish, Scotch-Irish, Osage, and Ponca Family Members at Buck Creek, Oklahoma

In 1934 Addison and Thelma Jump bought an eighty-acre meadow with arable land between Pawhuska and Bartlesville (on the Osage Reservation), a mile west of the one-room Buck Creek rural school that I would attend from 1936 to 1944. My mother had graduated in 1928 from Pawhuska High School (twenty miles west). Her father, James Alexander ("Aleck") Camp, was Scotch-Irish, his wife Sophronia Bell was Irish, and besides Thelma (b. 1908) they had six sons: Arthur (1898), Aubrey (1900), Bertrand (1904), Dwain (1906), Carter (1910), and Woodrow (1914). After Sophronia died in 1916, Alec took the children in a covered wagon to Oklahoma and found work in the oil-boom town of Pawhuska, where the Osage Tribal Agency was located.

Thelma Camp (top right) with basketball team, 1923.

Uncle Aubrey Camp,
wife Loretta, and son
Roy, c. 1928.

Maxine (left) and me at White Eagle, c. 1931–32.

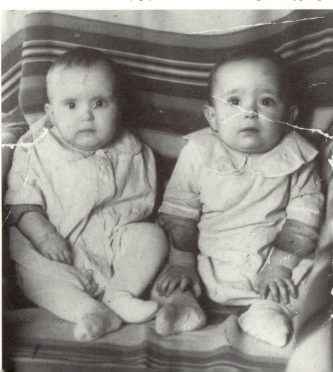

Family members after Aubrey's funeral, Buck Creek, 1934. I am at the left in the front row, and to my left are Roy Camp and Maxine Revard. In the second row, from left, are James Alexander Camp (grandfather), Aunt Jewell, Uncle Bert, Uncle Dwain, Aunt Loretta. In the back row are Uncle Woody, Uncle Carter, Addison Jump, and Thelma Jump, holding Ireta ("Josie").

Aunt Jewell and Addison standing with two Indian deputies (in hats) who had escorted Uncle Carter Camp from prison, where he was serving time for attempted bank robbery. Buck Creek, 1936.

The front steps of the house with some family members shortly before Uncle Carter Camp (center) was shot to death, Buck Creek, 1936. From left: Aunt Jewell McDonald Camp, cousin Roy Camp (top), Uncle Carter holding me, Thelma Jump holding Ireta ("Josie"), Loretta Camp (widow of Aubrey, mother of Roy), and Antwine in front.

In Buck Creek, on the same front steps and a year later. From left, they are Antwine, Maxine, me, and Uncle Dwain.

Buck Creek, 1936, behind the barn with a biplane often "parked" there by its owner, since he could land and take off on the half-mile of meadow there. Against the backdrop of Bockius's Hill to the west are Uncles Bert and Carter, Aunt Jewell, Uncle Woody, Roy, Maxine, Antwine, Thelma holding Ireta ("Josie"), and Addison.

An aerial view of the "horseless ranch" at Buck Creek, c. 1938.

Buck Creek, c. March 1941. In the back row are Thelma Jump holding her daughter Josephine, brother Antwine, sister Maxine, and Aunt Jewell. In the front row are brother Jim, cousins Dwain ("Bucky") and Darlena, sister Ireta ("Josie"), and me.

Roy Camp and his bride, Celestine Porter in California, c. 1942.

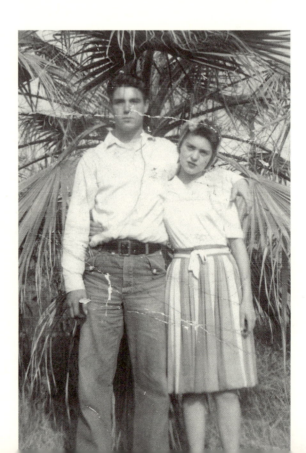

My brother Jim (right) and I,
Buck Creek, summer 1953.

Merton College Second Torpids Eight, Oxford, spring 1953. Back row: John Mays, Mark
Gretton, me, Stuart McGregor, Francis Allan. Second row: Colin Baker, Brian Mawer,
Anthony Littlewood, Ian McMichaels, Prosser Gifford. Seated front: coxwain William
Patchett. (Photo by Gilman & Soame Ltd., Oxford)

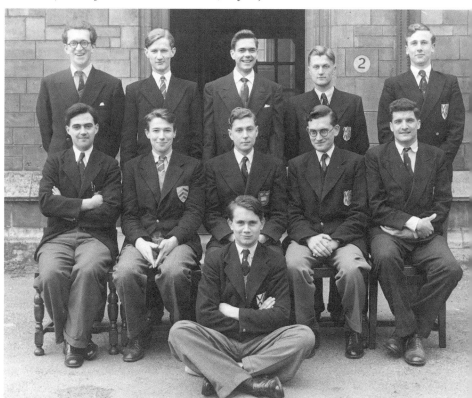

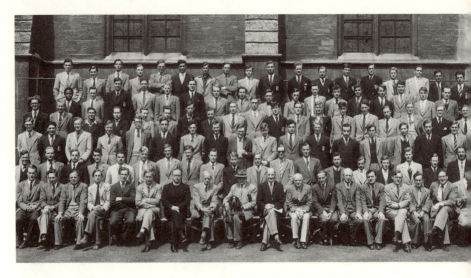

Students and faculty, Merton College, Oxford, 1952–53. The faculty, seated in front, included (seventh from right in the front row) J.R.R. Tolkien and (second right from Tolkien) another of the "Inklings," Hugo Dyson (my literary tutor). I am in the top row, third from right. (Photo by Gilman & Soame Ltd., Oxford)

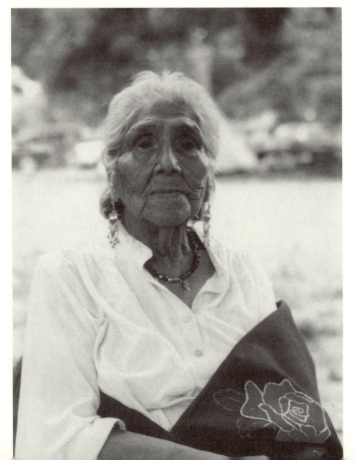

Aunt Jewell on family grounds at White Eagle, 1999.

26

Losses, Four

My twin sister Maxine made a great difference in my life when we were growing up. It is immensely helpful to have someone of the same age who can go along on just about any expedition, and knows all about you but still believes you are reasonably nice. She was a great help to me in grade school—whatever the grief, we could commiserate, whatever the fun, it was understood by the other— and we usually walked the mile to and from Buck Creek School together, often with other kids who would join us from where they lived in the hills to the north or south of Highway 60, which cut through the valley from east to west.

We had all the squabbling and selfish and silly disagreements that siblings have, and of course she went off and ran around with the girls and I with the boys a lot of the time too. At night all of us kids, including often our Ponca cousins who many times would be staying with us, would sit or lie around and tell stories, outrageous stories of enormous bears chasing the people we disliked at school, or those people coming to some comic and sometimes obscene end because of their own stupidity or misdoings. We would play cowboy and Indian games, Buck Rogers space-games, or just Buck Creek games: in the twilight yard, wood-tag among the fireflies; and in the summer moonlight out on the porch, there were old family stories from white uncles, and there might be songs from our Ponca aunt— who would sing us one we specially liked as a lullaby which many years later she told me was a "strongheart" song composed by her blind great-aunt to encourage her uncles after the Poncas were forced down from their home territory in Nebraska into Indian Territory in the late 1870s and 1880s. Its Ponca words put it very simply for the warriors, who were in despair and would take to drink to dull the despair: "What are you afraid of?" the song's words said: "No one can go around death."

Our last year at Buck Creek, in the eighth grade, Maxine and I took over the janitor chores, and would stay after school to sweep the floors, empty the wastebaskets and burn the trash, clean the blackboards and pound the chalk out of the erasers against the storm-cellar's barrel-shaped cement sides, as well as get there early to open and get things ready. We were paid nine dollars a month for this, and it seemed an enormous amount to have, when bread was a dime a loaf, bacon maybe twenty cents a pound, a hamburger no more than a dime. I suppose that nine dollars today would be worth ninety at least, and it helped keep us in less ragged clothes.

During high school, whenever I was not working with the greyhounds, we would usually catch a ride with neighbors taking their kids the five or six miles in to Bartlesville Central High and later College High—usually with Pat and Jimmie James, who lived up north of us and whose dad worked for Phillips Petroleum in Bartlesville. We would walk from our house up through the hay-meadow to the corner, rain or shine, burn or freeze, and wait for Mr. James to come barreling down from the hill in his 1938 Ford; then we'd climb in with his daughter Pat (same grade as us) and son Jimmie (three grades behind), and speed off to school.

In the tenth grade, Maxine began working in town weekdays after school and Saturdays—mostly in clothing stores, especially at Koppel's (women's clothing) near the old Osage Theater movie-house. When there was no greyhound work, I'd usually walk after school to the city library and read until my mother would get there to take us home, or until it was time to catch a ride back home with the neighbor kids. During greyhound-racing time I would ride to and from school with Johnny Kendall, and Maxine with our neighbors—or later, when we got a car running again to replace our old one that died during the last part of the war, with Mom.

When we started high school, we went from a rural one-room

school which had a total of thirteen children the year we graduated from its eighth grade, in to a three-story brick school which took up an entire block and had at least twelve hundred students. I probably could not have survived without my twin sister's help, mainly social but intellectual as well. She took Latin, and got straight A's in it; I took algebra, and got C and B. We both had good grades in other things, but the main thing was that I was pretty backward with girls, and since we were only thirteen—a year ahead of ourselves, having started school when we were five—I was small, and way behind the other boys in knowing how to talk and dress and act. Maxine advised on all fronts—teaching me for instance how to kiss a pillow semi-professionally even though when I actually got round to kissing my first date in the back of a car, it was remarkably different from kissing the pillow.

But in those days gender was fate more or less. Maxine took typing and shorthand, fell in love in her senior year and right after graduation married Tom Bailey and had two kids, went to work at Phillips Petroleum and never went on to college. We used to write back and forth now and then, and after I was teaching in the East I sent her some Oklahoma poems I had begun writing and she was the most favorable reader I could have had.

When they moved to California and lived out in the Oakland Bay area, she sent me some lovely prose about the country there, and who knows whether as the two boys got older she might not have got to writing things herself. But when we were only in our early thirties she was hit with ovarian cancer, and it took her very quickly, with barely time for me to get out and visit before she was gone. For two years I kept trying to write something for her, and couldn't find a good way; then on New Year's Eve of 1966–67, when I was visiting Professor Eikenberry at the University of Tulsa, by then long retired, I stayed up long after he had gone to bed, reading some things from Wordsworth and thinking New Year's thoughts, many of them about my sister, and near dawn it hit me how I might write something, which turned out to be "We Were Seven."

The title is a kind of rebuke directed at Wordsworth, who wrote a lovely poem called "We Are Seven," exalting a little girl who had been one of a family of seven children of whom one died, because when someone asked her how many children there were in her family, she replied simply "We Are Seven," implying that the death made no difference to their being together. I felt so lost without my sister, so like a moon that had lost its atmosphere, that I wanted to just insist to Wordsworth: No, we WERE seven, now we are SIX kids in our family.

But here is the poem:

We Were Seven

—I must have developed kind of late, sexually.
Well, I chased after several redlipped girls,
But got a lot more pleasure, aged fourteen,
From a redbellied woodpecker I saw one day
Off in the woods. Our bio-teacher told us
Redbellied woodpeckers never came to Oklahoma,
Not to our part at least. I saw one, though,
When we were cutting hearthwood down by Buck Creek,
And by God no other woodpecker looks like that—
Tightfitting cap of red clear down his nape,
Black and white ladder-speckles down his back.
The funny thing, was Mr. Shamberger never questioned
My mockingbird reports, and *they* later turned out
A nest of shrikes. It's not too easy, finding
A bird that looks just like its picture but not
Just *almost* like some damn Brazilian species.

—In California, all that milk and honey,
When my twin sister was going to die with cancer,
She asked me pointblank, "Mike, you believe in God?"
She'd kept trying to reform me since, at thirteen,
I said there *was* no God. Well, no use lying
To somebody that always sees you blush about it—
So I just told her, "No, I really don't,"
Then lied about expecting her to live.

Which didn't matter—she knew damn well she wouldn't.
Well, H. Earl Shamberger had got it wrong—
Redbellied woodpeckers live in Oklahoma.
No reason a bird of paradise can't visit our yard;
It'll have a legband saying, *Wish you were here.*
I keep close watch on all the trees we have.

27

Family Values
Bankrobbing

When we had first moved out to Buck Creek, the photographs show Maxine and me as nearly always together, and through the first grade of school often in almost identical outfits, overalls or whatever. There are pictures, for instance, from the occasion of our Uncle Aubrey's funeral, that first summer we were living out at Buck Creek. He had done some bootlegging, and had an attitude, which got him beaten to death in the Pawhuska jail by one of the meaner policemen there. After the funeral in Pawhuska the folks gathered over at Buck Creek and pictures were taken with the old Eastman Kodak which my mother and Addison had bought.

In the pictures, we are assembled on the front porch steps of the Buck Creek house, in the strong summer sunlight: Grandpa Camp, Uncle Bert back from his time in prison for bootlegging, Uncle Carter out on parole from his prison sentence for robbing a bank, Uncle Dwain back from his Army service in the Philippines, Addison and my mother (she holding my little sister Ireta, a baby of five or six months), Uncle Woody and his new wife Aunt Jewell, Uncle Aubrey's widow Loretta. Standing among them, or sitting, or held by one of the uncles or by Aunt Jewell in different pictures, are Maxine and me, our older brother Antwine, and our cousin Roy.

In one of those pictures, as Aunt Jewell has told me, there are Indians from four different tribes: herself (Ponca), Addison (Osage), and two deputies who had escorted our Uncle Carter from his prison to the funeral and who would be escorting him back—the deputies being from two other tribes, which Aunt Jewell has named for me but which I forget. In that picture, the deputies wear Stetson hats and look with amused confidence into the camera, Addison stands shyly aloof as usual, and Aunt Jewell is cutting her eyes in distrust toward the two deputies.

Uncle Carter, in many of those pictures, is wearing a big white Stetson hat and a sleek dark suit and tie: when I asked Mom, years later, how come he got into all that robbery and stuff, she said in disgusted bemusement: "He always had to have the best clothes there were." When those pictures were taken, he was just allowed out of prison long enough to come to the funeral, but a couple of years later he actually was paroled, and he came to live with us for the summer before he was killed.

The family story about his robbing the bank and getting shot and captured always began by telling what kind of man he was. Born in 1910 and thus two years younger than our mother, he was only four when his mother died, and only six or so when Grandpa moved the family to Pawhuska. There, he went to school, but it was a roistering oil-boom town and he was more often out of school than in it—and, big for his age, smart and aggressive, he got into trouble early and often.

My cousin Roy, who saw a lot of his Uncle Carter (only fifteen when Roy was born), tells me he was hell on wheels in a fight, and speaks of one occasion at a carnival to which Uncle Carter had taken Roy and his mom Loretta and my mother (Carter's big sister). One of the carnival guys in some way insulted my mother, and Carter decked him. The guy, being one of the carnies, yelled out "Hey, Rube," and a slew of carnival workers came running up and pitched into Uncle Carter. Roy, who was then maybe five years old, says it was amazing to hear Carter's fists hitting those guys, it was like an axe chopping oak logs. He says three of them were on the ground before they knew it, then another one hit Carter over the head from behind with a one-inch steel pipe and staggered him, just as Uncle Aubrey came running up and pitched in, and it was Katie bar the door, or rather Shut the door, they're coming in the windows, shut the windows, they're coming in the door. Luckily a swarm of local police came up and sorted them out—apparently just giving Uncle Carter and family the bum's rush off the carnival grounds, where the bruises and cuts were dealt with in the old-fashioned way, with a little water and a lot of home brew.

So, with a champagne appetite and home brew income, Uncle Carter wanted the best, and did not care how he got the money for it. He had been up to quite a bit of illegal stuff, bootlegging and worse, from his teens on. About 1930, though—when he was twenty or so—he had been persuaded by his father, Grandpa Camp, to go straight, and was getting ready to move down to Alabama or Mississippi and start over on the straight side. But while he was getting ready to go he was still doing some partying, and he was always a ladies' man. The place where he was staying belonged to a fairly big bootlegger—that is, one who was in good with the cops supposed to be policing him. And this bootlegger had a pretty young wife who got sweet on Uncle Carter, and he did not put her off, and they had some pretty good times.

But the bootlegger was no fool, he caught on—and instead of saying anything and maybe getting the hell beat out of him, he cooked up a good revenge scheme. He told Uncle Carter there was this bank over in Marland that was an easy place to knock over, and since Carter was going to head down to Alabama to go straight, he could take some of the bank's cash with him to help get started down there. So Carter and the guy that was going to go to Alabama with him fell for this scheme and they made plans for the robbery. However, the bootlegger quietly tipped the police, not using his phone but that of a neighbor lady who was supposed to be old and never would notice what he was saying. He gave the police all the details of what day and what time, what kind of guns and how many robbers there would be, and he gave them their names. This would let the police catch the bankrobbers and look good, and it would get the bootlegger in even more solidly with the police so he could run his stuff even more profitably, and everybody would come out ahead except Uncle Carter and his colleague.

The understanding was that the cops would wait in ambush across the street from the bank, in this little three-street town of Marland, which mostly consisted of a grain elevator (in prime wheat country) next to a railroad, with a store, a bank, and maybe at that time actually a movie, plus a few hundred people. And when Carter and his buddy came out of the bank with the loot, they would be shot dead: that was the reasonable plan.

It worked beautifully, or almost. The other guy fell dead at the first fusillade, but Carter was very smart, realized at once it was a setup, took a bullet to his hip and went down, and played dead so successfully that the cops thought he was finished. They had an ambulance—already waiting, I think—which they called on in. However, after they had dumped the other guy and Carter into the back of the ambulance, and were driving them on up to Ponca City—to the morgue, as they thought—the policeman riding in the ambulance got to talking with the driver, and started bragging about how the police and their friends had set up this robbery and how the damn fool robbers had walked out of the bank right into their bullets. Whereupon Uncle Carter sat up and said to the driver and his helper in back with him, "Look, I'm alive, and I heard that, and so did the both of you." The cop wanted to shoot him again, but the driver and helper said they couldn't go along because there were people back there who knew Carter had only been shot once, and so on.

The result was that they rushed Carter in to the Ponca City Hospital, he survived, and at his trial had expected to beat the rap because it was a case of entrapment to which he had witnesses. By that time he knew about the old lady whose phone the bootlegger used to talk with the police, and she was supposed to be a corroborating witness.

But when it came time for the trial, for some reason neither the ambulance driver nor his helper could be found to testify, and the old lady had died. So Carter was found guilty and sentenced to a term in the state prison at McAlester. It was from there that he was brought up to Pawhuska for the funeral of his brother, Uncle Aubrey, by the two Indians serving as deputies to escort him.

I still wonder how Carter ever got paroled as soon as he did. He was not in jail more than five years, maybe only four, before they paroled him. And once he was out at our place, it became apparent that he had in mind some other ways of getting rich quickly. This

was the summer of 1936, and we were out at Buck Creek, in a
terribly dry year, and Uncle Carter, and Grandpa, and our stepfather Addison, and Mom, always seemed to have plenty to do.

Grandpa and the uncles had built a barbed-wire fence around
the eighty acres, and a cow-pond down in the swale, and another
fence which bisected the pond so horses and cattle could be kept in
the big pasture, while the smaller meadow and arable part could be
sown to barley or oats or corn. And they had cut postoak saplings
and built stalls in the cowbarn, and we were baling two or three
thousand bales of the best prairie hay off the meadow each year, and
we had a hoglot, and milk cows, and beef cattle, a pair of work
horses and a pair of mules, a pinto half-Arabian mare named Beauty
for saddle horse. Then after Carter was there a month or so there
seemed to be money to buy more cattle, and he bought a police dog
(German shepherd) to kennel next to our chicken house, so as to
keep thieves and coyotes and maybe skunks and weasels away from
the gamecocks and laying chickens there—not to mention the calves
and pigs.

It was exciting to have Uncle Carter there, that summer when
I was five years old. I can remember his being there when the bluestem meadow, despite the Dust Bowl heat and drought, had got up
knee-high and was all green and full of meadowlarks and bobwhites,
and how Uncle Carter got me out there one morning early and said
he was going to teach me to ride and we would see how fast old
Beauty could run. She was a fleet thing, built like a quarter-horse
but with the Arabian's more delicate head and legs and a fine
flowing tail and mane to go with her white and rufous brown
camouflage coat.

Uncle Carter cinched the saddle tight, and lifted me up where
I could grab the saddlehorn and hold on for dear life, then he stuck
his left foot in the stirrup and swung a leg over, and Beauty shivered
and pranced and I thought sure I'd be thrown, and he put his
arms on either side of me and slacked the reins and said "C'mon,
little Painted Baby" and she took off across that half-mile of green
meadow like a bear was behind her. Uncle Carter didn't pull on the
reins till we were getting up near the north fence, and then he
pulled her around to the left, and she galloped a couple of hundred

yards up near the western fence, and he reined her left again and pulled her back to a lope, and then a trot, which I hated because it was hard on my bottom and also kept me feeling ready to tip or slide off. But by the time we got back to the house I had caught on a little and was not quite so scared, just wishing we'd stop and I could get off.

As it happened that was the only ride I had with him. Not so long afterward he went out into the night, singing a song then popular, and got himself shot to death trying to hijack a shipment of extra-good bootleg whisky that the Kansas City mob (supposedly) was running down into Oklahoma: although by 1936 Prohibition had been ended nationally, Oklahoma was still dry and would remain so till the 1960s.

28

Losses, Five

A long time later—in 1969–70—I wrote a poem for Uncle Carter, which was published in the anthology *Voices of the Rainbow* (Viking Press, 1975). After it had come out, I was invited to give a reading at the University of Oklahoma by Alan Velie and his doctoral student Norma Wilson, and this was one of the poems I read then. After the reading, a woman came up to me and said that was an interesting story about my bankrobbing uncle, and just that morning she had been stripping the cover and padding off an old ironing board and found inside as part of the padding some pages of an old newspaper from about 1930, in which there was an account of a bank robbery which sounded kind of like the one my Uncle Carter had taken part in. She showed me the piece of newspaper, and it was about my Uncle Carter's bank robbery and trial. So here is the poem: its title reflects a Nixonian bumper-sticker from the years 1968–70, "Support Your Local Police."

Support Your Local Police Dog

The night before Uncle Carter got shot dead
Trying to hijack a load of bootleg whisky,
He dressed fit to kill, put on his lilac hairoil
And leaned down to the mirror in our living room
To comb the hair back over his bald spot, humming,
"Corinne, Corin-ne, where have you been so long?"

I don't know if "Corinne" tipped the other bunch off,
But I hope he made it with her before they killed him.
I bet if there was any, he was getting his—
Jesus, I never saw him standing still
Or lying down, till they led me past his coffin.
He should've been born a lord in Boswell's time,
Though he'd most likely been laid up with gout
Before he was forty, had that uric drive.
More drive than brains, though. Hell, out on parole
For robbing a bank, his hip not very long healed
Where the cop in ambush shot him trying to surrender,
Had no more sense than go after those bottled-in-bonders
From Kansas City? You *know* they'd be in cahoots
With local crooks and laws. We couldn't see why
A man with his brains ever got talked into trying.
My Uncle Dwain said must've been a put-up job,
He knew too much, the gang'd had him bumped off.
Well, the last time I was home for a visit,
Our Oklahoma voters had just made whisky legal,
But I'd been living with earnest city people
That keep *discovering* crime and poverty
Like tin cans tied to their suburbs' purebred tails
Till they run frothing, yapping for law and order,
So turning from U.S. Sixty off to our house,
I thought of the big police dog Carter brought home
His last time there, and kennelled by the chickenhouse.
Nobody was going to steal our stock, by God.
—Later, the damn dog got to killing turkeys
On a neighbor's place; we had to let it be shot.
The gilt mirror Carter peered at his bald spot in
Had been demoted, now hung dim in the bathroom.
I patted the Old Spice lather on and shaved
As suavely as he had combed, and smelled as good—
He never lived to grow white whiskers like mine.
I knew the smartest crooks don't ever need guns,
And I would never walk out into the night

To get myself shot down, the way he did.
I've got more brains. But while he lived, I admit,
He was my favorite uncle: guts, charm, and drive.
He would have made a perfect suburban mayor—
Or later, manager for some liquor chain.

29

Indian Survival, Two

I guess if Uncle Carter had been a woman we could call his activities "transgressional" and discuss them as ways of resisting the
patriarchal culture. If he were put into a Marxist story he could be
an example of how capitalism creates great social chasms by
inequitable distribution of wealth, or maybe how proletarian violence
is a response to the imposition of class barriers and is a mistaken
form of class struggle, since the proper response would be to confi-
scate the wealth not by private criminal enterprise but by public
revolutionary seizure. Kind of hard to imagine how to tell his story
had I framed him as Irish and Scotch-Irish, but he might look good
in Appalachian Orange as a Jesse James figure, or in Potato Patch
Green as an IRA man in the wrong time and place. I suppose H. L.
Mencken would have viewed him as among the natural results of
Bible-belted Bluenose Prohibition Mentality. He could be fitted into
a nice bourgeois account by assuming his position as White Trash,
that is, bent over and waiting for the forces of Law and Order to
apply the usual punishment.

On the other hand, if a whole country goes to war, it sends
hordes of young men over into neighboring territories—or even
territories on the other side of the world—to take over all the places
in those territories including their banks. We send them, that is, to
do something like what Uncle Carter was doing, and we give them
medals for murdering other men, or for that matter women and
children (by indiscriminately bombing, or by inadvertently shooting
them while aiming at "soldiers"). It interests me very much that a

lot of American Indians have taken part in American wars as a way of showing support of the nation which has become the official guardian of Indian peoples. As I have been told, and I tend to believe, the relative numbers of Indian people who have served in American wars is very high, and some people say we are the most active of all "ethnic groups," percentagewise, in wars of this century.

It's one way to survive, after all. For a long time, military service has seemed to offer entry into the American "mainstream"—just as in the Roman Empire, citizenship could be obtained by being a member of a Roman legion, even if you were a Gaul or Dalmatian or Iberian or whatever. My Osage Uncle Kenneth served for instance in the Pacific campaigns of World War Two, and was active later in the Pawhuska (Osage) post of the American Legion, serving as Commander for a time. When I was given my Osage name in 1952, the feast and handgames and dance were held, I think, in the American Legion Hall there in Pawhuska.

Years later in St. Louis—maybe 1978—members of our Indian Community took part, one spring, in a parade organized in support of the Veterans of Foreign Wars. We had lately formed an Indian Center and begun putting on powwows in St. Louis, and a lot of our dancers and singers were veterans. The powwow is a way of survival: a form of lasting communal action by which to recover our place which otherwise would have been taken away by the Empire. Dancing, singing, writing are among the more peaceful ways to reclaim our place. Cliff Walker, the Omaha chair of our Powwow Committee, was a WWII veteran who had for thirty years worked at the U.S. Army's supply center in St. Louis, and many of our Indian Community people were veterans of WWII, of Korea, of Vietnam.

So when the local chapter of Veterans of Foreign Wars invited us to take part, to bring a kind of float to their parade, we were glad to be asked. One of the Community members had access to a big flatbed truck, and our local Drum (the term refers to both singers and drum) and some of our dancers and women in their outfits— Gourd Dance, "straight," "traditional," and "fancy wardance" regalia, and the women in shawls and maybe white buckskin— would ride on the flatbed, and the rest of us in our outfits would walk behind. Those on the flatbed held up a big banner announcing our powwow to be held in June in Jefferson Barracks Park, in south St. Louis.

That park, as mentioned in the poem, is where the Dragoons were quartered for the Indian Wars beginning in the 1830s. A great many veterans are buried there from the various wars from then to now, and starting with World War One a considerable number of these are American Indians. Our early powwows were held on other grounds, and it gave real satisfaction when some of our Indian Community people with friends in the Park Service were able to talk the Jefferson Barracks people into letting us dance there.

There was a fair amount of reluctance based on the perception of Indians as radical AIM members prone to violence, or alcoholic troublemakers in general. The general view I sensed among people I have dealt with over the years—particularly when in 1985 I had to persuade Washington University people to let us hold a mini-powwow using Missouri Humanities money in a W.U. building—is that Indians are apt to leave a big mess, being dirty and slovenly and obviously just a poorer class of people: why else would they live in such appalling conditions on their reservations, or come into the city and be so irresponsibly poor and helpless?

So to dance in the green and pleasant confines of Jefferson Barracks Park, overlooking the great rolling Mississippi, under pines and tulip and sweetgum and oak trees, with room for the traders' booths and for the visiting Indian families from Arizona and New Mexico and Oklahoma and Kansas and Nebraska and the Dakotas, maybe down from Wisconsin and up from Mississippi and Louisiana, over from Illinois and Indiana—that was a kind of sweet survival statement by those against whom the Dragoons had made war to cleanse the Manifestly Destined United States of our kind forever.

And of course the rest of the poem is very close to how it was. It is almost a "found poem," because it simply reports what we did and what took place. But I thought it carried a good deal of resonance, and it has seemed to wake up some of my academic friends in a gentle way.

Parading with the Veterans of Foreign Wars

Apache, Omaha, Osage, Choctaw, Comanche, Cherokee, Oglala,
    Micmac:
our place was ninety-fifth,
and when we got there with our ribbon shirts
and drum and singers on the trailer,
women in shawls and traditional dresses,
we looked into the muzzle of
an Army howitzer in front of us.
"Hey, Cliff," I said,
"haven't seen guns that big
since we were in Wounded Knee."
Cliff carried the new American flag
donated by another post; Cliff prays
in Omaha for us, being chairman
of our Powwow Committee, and his prayers
keep us together, helped
by hard work from the rest of course.
"They'll move that one-oh-five ahead," Cliff said.
They did, but then the cavalry arrived.
No kidding, there was this troop outfitted
with Civil War style uniforms and carbines,
on horseback, metal clopping on
the asphalt street, and there
on jackets were the insignia:
the Seventh Cavalry, George Custer's bunch.
"Cliff," Walt said, "they think you're Sitting Bull."
"Just watch out where you're stepping, Walt,"
Cliff said, "Those pooper-scoopers
will not be working when the parade begins."
"Us women walking behind the trailer
will have to step around it all
so much, they'll think we're dancing,"
was all that Sherry said.
We followed
the yellow line, and here and there

some fake war-whoops came out to us
from sidewalk faces, but applause
moved with us when the singers started,
and we got our banners seen announcing
this year's Powwow in June,
free to the public in Jefferson Barracks Park—
where the Dragoons were quartered for the Indian Wars.
When we had passed the Judging Stand
and pulled off to the little park all
green and daffodilly under the misting rain,
we put the shawls and clothing in the cars
and went back to the Indian Center, while
Cliff and George Coon went out and got
some chicken from the Colonel
that tasted great, given the temporary
absence of buffalo here in the
Gateway to the West, St. Louis.

Maybe some local and even personal history will be helpful
here. In 1972 and 1973 there were uprisings in Indian Country, and
members of the American Indian Movement were at the forefront
of these uprisings. I have six cousins who are half-Ponca, children
of my beloved Ponca Aunt Jewell and her late husband, my Irish
and Scotch-Irish Uncle Woody Camp. My Ponca cousin Carter
Camp was a national leader of AIM who fought in the two most
publicized battles of that time: the takeover in October/November
1972 of the Bureau of Indian Affairs building in Washington, D.C.,
and the occupation of Wounded Knee from March to early May
of 1973.

My Osage brother Addison Jump also took part in the Washington, D.C., action, but then said the hell with it and went back to
teaching math at Haskell Indian College in Lawrence, Kansas.
Addison later resigned the Haskell job and joined the Defense
Department as computer programmer and mathematical analyst,
one of those who have taught the Tomahawk missiles to take the
proper scalps; for some years he has lived in the Virginia countryside south of Washington, D.C.

Traditional Indian people all across the United States and in other nations took keen notice of the AIM actions. The "short-hairs" of the BIA, who often were heads of tribal government and controllers of patronage with Washington pipelines, usually hung back from or opposed the "militant" AIM warriors. But all Indian people understood then and now that things "on the Rez" are far from ideal and that some of the reasons for this include racism and corruption both within official tribal governments and all through the interfaces with local and national Anglo government.

By 1972, Indian people had watched the Civil Rights uprisings, had seen the federal government respond with at least some gestures toward help and support of Martin Luther King and others. Many Indian people thought it was well past time that Indians stood up for their rights, and called for federal help against oppressive local and state officials, whether the sheriffs and judges and lawyers, or the ranchers and bankers and rednecks who were often the same people or from the same circles and families as those controlling local justice and law enforcement and finances.

So when AIM and others called for Indian people to come along to Washington in 1972 on a walk called the "Trail of Broken Treaties," Indian people from a great many reservations and tribal areas joined that walk, and at first the Nixon administration seemed willing to talk the talk if not walk the walk with them. Haldeman and Ehrlichman and John Mitchell and Gordon Liddy, and all the Watergate boys whose high crimes and misdemeanors would presently bring down Tricky Dicky, had not yet been exposed, and the Nixonians did not want any bad press involving Indian people. Nixon himself had voiced reasonable policies, had no sinister feelings about or views of Indians, would in fact help the Pueblos recover Blue Lake and Jim Thorpe recover his decathlon medal. So it looked good for the Trail of Broken Treaties in 1972.

I won't try to explain how the walk got infiltrated, how the Nixonians betrayed the causes and the people, how the promises were not kept, how the places promised for the Indian people to stay in Washington had rats and no toilets or whatever. Nor will I tell some of the stories from my cousin Carter and brother Addison about their going to the BIA building in an effort to get some improvement in the housing and a hearing about the problems which the Longest Walk people had come to discuss, or stories about taking over the Bureau of Indian Affairs building—the rough confrontations, doublecrosses, buying off and selling out and getting the people back to their reservations by hook or crook or practical dealmaking.

Nor will I tell much of the return to reservations, the sitting down and talking with tribal elders about what was actually intended and really accomplished, or how—on some reservations—U.S.-backed tribal governments tried to prevent such communication between traditional Indians who wanted a firsthand account and hoped to question carefully the AIM people to see whether they were pinko alcoholic druggie and Commie off-reservation subversives, as painted by the Nixonian and FBI and other sources, or were real Indians trying to get solutions to problems all the Indians understood were real and urgent. My view is the latter, and I would give a historical account based on that view.

Here, the point is just that such confrontations, after the AIM people got back from the BIA takeover, tied in with violent efforts by U.S.-backed groups to suppress not only AIM people but any supporters of them, using strongarm tactics—beating, shooting, provocations, threatening—and that on the Pine Ridge Reservation some traditional people asked the AIM warriors to help them resist this, which led to the AIM takeover of the Wounded Knee site and trading post on the last day of February in 1973.

Three of my Ponca cousins took part in the Wounded Knee occupation, and I myself got inside very briefly—during my midsemester break from teaching at Washington University, St. Louis. A movie called *Lakota Woman* came out in 1995, much of it dealing with the 1972–73 events and their aftermath in which my cousin Carter played a leading role. In the movie, the actor who plays the role of Carter is a younger man, a Pawnee and Yuchi artist and photographer named Richard Ray Whitman, while Carter himself was filmed for the movie riding a beautiful paint pony and wearing a headdress, but the shot was cut from the final version. Richard

Whitman was actually a lieutenant of Carter's, and when Carter
finally surrendered at Wounded Knee and was helicoptered out in
chains and handcuffs, he turned authority over to Richard.

Since I was teaching my classes at Washington University in
St. Louis during the final part of the Wounded Knee occupation, I
was asked by the media people there to come on talk radio and a few
TV programs to speak of what was happening, and to take questions;
I was liaison with some of the AIM people occupying Wounded Knee
who were able to slip out through the military cordon or were
allowed to come out and speak, and who appeared with me on KMOX
for instance. This meant that a lot of Indian people in the St. Louis
area got in touch with me, people I had not met. (There were also a
large number of narcs pretending to be Indian who kept trying to
get in with me and wanted me to come over and have a joint or meet
this beautiful blonde groupie who was dying to express her approval
of Indian spirituality and her love for the great bronze warriors of
AIM. Luckily I can't stand pot and am not bronze.)

Among them were Indian people who had moved, or been
moved, to St. Louis during the Eisenhower administration's effort
toward a final solution of the Indian Problem by getting them all
into cities where there were jobs and they could become civilized.
There were Comanche and Omaha and Seneca and Cherokee and
Kiowa and Arikawa and other people whom I met during 1973–74,
while we were engaged among other things in trying to help AIM
members and their families through the time after Wounded Knee,
while the federal prosecutions and persecutions were at their height,
and there were people in jail or on probation for whom bail money,
jobs, or help for pregnant wives or children, was needed.

So about February 1974 some of us put an ad in the paper
inviting all St. Louis area Indian people to come and meet and get
to know each other and see whether we might organize an Indian
Center to help deal with the kinds of difficulties people were going
through here, and to find ways of educating the non-Indian people
of good will about who we were, what we are, and how the rest of
the community might better understand and better relate to our
Indian people. This meeting and others did get such an Indian
Center set up, incorporated, and housed in a succession of cheap

rented places. Because I was out of the country from July 1974 to
September 1975 I was not there when the actual setting up, writing
the bylaws, and incorporating were accomplished, and I did not get
involved with the new center's activities until the winter of 1975–76
and then only by going along to meetings and a dance or two. But
in early June 1976 the first ever St. Louis Indian Powwow was
held, and as a member of the Powwow Committee I was active in
trying to raise the funds needed for this—my English Department
colleagues now saw me as not only a nut but a nuisance trying to
sell them raffle tickets on shawls and blankets and bracelets. I
quickly decided to buy all the raffle tickets I could afford and then
a lot more, and give these away as unthreateningly as possible to
colleagues who did not bristle at the very thought of having anything to do with any faintly subversive Indian affair whatever.

It was much like helping raise money for a charity ball, or a
heart fund, or whatever. Much worse than being the United Way
rep. And of course that first powwow was an unimpressive affair:
ourselves, a few friends who came to dance with us from their reservations in Oklahoma or South Dakota or Nebraska or Kansas, or
their tribal areas elsewhere, and a few curious and critical non-
Indian spectators. By then all the factional and personal feuds
expected in a Poetry Society or an English Department or even a
Medical School had broken out and I knew a little more about where
the emotional and tribal minefields were located in the community.

I stayed away from Board meetings, which I heard were
usually like negotiations between the PLO and Israel, and remained
friends with both groups—or, more accurately since the Board then
had about eight members I think, with *all forty* groups of Board
members (each member constituted at least one group, but also
belonged to at least one and as many as seven other groups so far as
I could understand it). And in the summer of 1976 I was again overseas, in England for medieval research which would occupy much
of my summers for the next twenty years and sometimes part of the
academic year as well. But each year thereafter I was active in the
Indian Center's work and play, socializing with the other Indian
people in the community, and starting in 1975–76 to learn much
more about traditional Indian ways.

162 Indian Survival, Two

When the Kiowa and Comanche people of the area formed a Gourd Dance group, I was invited to become one of the dancers, was taught some of the lore and customs and background of the Gourd Dance (it comes from the Kiowa and Comanche people, among whom a Gourd Dancer is a warrior). We were taught how to make our gourds, and some of us learned to do the beadwork (sewing the tiny glass beads onto the handles of gourds or of fans, or onto the medallions and parts of the dance regalia), and we strung our bandoliers of silver beads and mescal berries, we were given our Gourd Dance blankets and sashes and we made our medicine bundles to pin to our shirts for the dances. I learned a little of the Gourd Dance songs, and learned to dance the right steps at the right time, and I bought the standard items—cowboy boots, a cowboy hat, the proper colored shirts, and neat trousers. Because I did not have any hawk or eagle feathers, I had to ask my Ponca cousins for a fan to carry, and my Ponca cousin Casey's husband Mike beaded me a very beautiful fan of a redtail hawk's tail. I bought a carefully shaped gourd-handle of persimmon wood, and Mike made me a gourd with fine beadwork. Some of the "gourds" are made of saltshakers or peppershakers, with small shot or with stones to make them rattle; mine was a real gourd, a small one, dried and with tiny stones in it.

We would assemble, have dinner at the house of one of our Gourd Dance group, or at a hall where we would be holding the dance, and we would listen to one of those with knowledge of the songs and of the Gourd Dance customs and their meanings, and our singers would drum and sing a set of eight songs and we would dance there, with those of us learning to dance watching and occasionally asking for help or information from those who knew the ways. Every once in a while during the winter a fund-raising dance might be held, and donations of money or of things that could be sold to raise money took place.

The fund-raising had to cover travel and lodging of the Drum (singers who bring the drum), the prize money for contest winners, food for Drum, dancers and guests, maybe rental fees of the place where the dance is held, for janitors and cleanup people if it's held in a university gymnasium. One source of funds is the Powwow Traders who bring their wares for sale around the powwow grounds or hall. Each of these will pay a certain amount for booth space, but they will not come to a powwow where the spectators and potential buyers of the goods are few. So if we want to charge forty or fifty traders fifty or a hundred dollars for a booth, they have to expect to sell enough to pay for their expenses and make a profit. That means we have to publicize, and to draw a good many non-Indian people who will want to buy genuine Indian wares—and I have to add that making sure these *are* Indian wares, made and sold by really Indian people, is part of our job in organizing a powwow. It is easier to sell booth space to non-Indians pushing kitsch which sells big, than space to real Indians with shawls and beadwork and art they have made and want to sell at a decent price.

We hoped our powwows would also bring non-Indians to have a good time and learn something of Indian people, and to buy genuine Indian things from those who made them. That would be doing something for Indian *and* non-Indian community, as well as having ourselves a fine time, and keeping some of our Indian ways and understanding, and for that matter making our footsteps prayers for the well-being of our relatives and friends. And if we could do better financially than break even on the whole powwow, this would be used toward the next year's event, or could become part of the food pantry and help toward financial or other problems of members of the Indian community.

That's a long and tedious account: yet it might serve to let non-Indians see a little behind the scenes as it were, get a sense that like a presidential nominating convention, or an MLA convention, Indian gatherings take more than a few "ugh!" and "how!" expressions to put together.

30

Indian Survival, Three
In and Out of Las Vegas

There seem to be, lately, a lot of white people trying to save Indians from the evils of gambling, especially after they notice that Indians are making a lot of money from all the white people flocking to the tribal casinos. On one occasion, I was told by friends, Andy Rooney, at the end of a *Sixty Minutes* program, expressed grave concern at the corruption of Indian character revealed by this gambling craze, and offered some excellent advice on how to follow the example of white people and become television pundits—advice which I wish I had heard, but it happened I was out of the house that night and did not get to benefit by it. The next week, though, I tuned in and heard Mr. Rooney complain that a lot of Indian people had written him nasty letters about his wise words. One of those letter-writers was quoted by another of the program's sages as suggesting that an Irishman should first try to straighten out the Irish before starting in on the Indians.

Ah well now, being part Irish but never the bit of a gambler, it's I in faith who must sympathize with Andy and all the O'Rooneys in their desire to moralize the Indian part of me, which if I let it go would doubtless drag me through meadow and bog in search of a fourleaf clover, shamrock I mean!—that I could take to the nearest casino, where I would ask for cup after cup of poteen while I gambled away the money my poor abused wife would be spending on commodity cheese and powdered milk for the horde of squalling savage children back home in the tepee. Had I not noticed long ago, indeed, when I was a lad in Pawhuska, that whenever our Osage and other Indian people were playing handgames of an evening there, some of the fullblood elders would be betting each other which hand the bead was in? It was proof positive, it was, that the gambling virus was not of European origin, and was in the Indian blood, indeed, indeed.

On the other hand, I have noticed that not all persons of European origins seem immune to the gambling virus. About 1979, in a visit to Las Vegas for strictly professional purposes—namely, to give a paper at a session of the Rocky Mountain Modern Language Association—I was told by a reliable source that the whole state of Nevada depended heavily for its public revenues on gambling and prostitution, and yet the other members of Congress did not bar the Nevada senator and representatives from taking their seats and offering legislation, even legislation involving gambling.

Further research has shown that in a town called Atlantic City there have been for some years white people addicted to gambling, the vice Indians have lately given a bad name. There seems to be a man named Donald Trump who owns a great casino there, and perhaps also owns a Congressman or two—none of them a member of any Indian tribe so far as I know. These Congressmen seem louder even than Mr. Rooney in preaching to the poor benighted Indians the evils of gambling. Or perhaps that misrepresents the Trump Doctrine, which holds that the casinos in Connecticut and Massachusetts, which appear to be doing better than those of Trump, are owned by Indians who do not look Indian, being blacker or whiter than Indians ought to be.

These grave concerns come to mind when I remember the two occasions I was in Las Vegas. The first was back in 1968, when I was also there for professional reasons. Having spent a year and a half, funded by the Department of Defense (through ARPA), in cramming a dictionary into computers and trying to get it out again, I was in Las Vegas to give a paper on some of the results to the Association for Computational Machinery's convention there in August 1968. Because my personal part of the travel and lodging expenses were paid for, I could afford a room in Caesar's Palace for

Stella and the three children we then had, and once the computer/ dictionary paper was delivered we had a short while to see how the white people gambled in the proper ways, and what kind of buildings they had constructed in which to do that and other things which they would later be warning Indians not to do.

Stella (who is half Irish) had taken an oath never to gamble, years before, on the condition that at any time when she wanted to get a ticket to an opera there would be one she could get; and since that condition had been fully met ever since, she had never gambled since that time. Myself, I had seen some uncles lose enough by things near enough to gambling that I would not do it at all. This left us with very little to do in Las Vegas except watch the other people doing what we would not. So after we had put the kids to sleep about ten o'clock on our last night in Caesar's Palace, we left them up in the room and went downstairs to live high for a half hour or so. We went into what seemed to be a soda fountain or milk bar part and recklessly ordered a pineapple malt for me and a hot chocolate for Stella, and settled back to case the joint.

The first thing we saw, not far away at the end of the bar—and drinking what looked suspiciously like sarsaparilla—was Somebody Famous, a real TV Star—Ed Sullivan, in fact (the name sounds Irish, but what would an Irishman have been doing in such a gambling joint?). Now, we both saw him, and looked at each other, and had the same thought: back in St. Louis, where we were headed, our babysitter for some years had been a beautiful middle-aged woman, Mary Hutchinson, née Sullivan. She loved Ed Sullivan's show, and if we could get his autograph to her.... At a nod from Stella, I set down my malt-glass and started toward Mr. Sullivan. Now he, out of the corner of his eye, recognized an autograph hound heading his way, and a little dimple came out on the left side of his face—not a smile, he was being modest, but an expression that said, "A fan has seen me, I will be gracious."

Unfortunately, as I stepped aside to let somebody past me, my eye fell on someone else sitting at a table off to my left, just beyond Sullivan. It was the great boxer, Joe Louis, leaning back in his chair and looking a little nervous. This was the real thing, and I lost all interest in a mere TV star, moving on past him toward the Louis table.

As I passed Sullivan, I saw his cheek tighten and his eye narrow: he realized he had been dumped, and I probably could not have got an autograph from him at that point. As I walked diffidently by him, Louis saw me coming—and without looking at me tightened himself as if I might be a threat of some kind. I stopped a little way from the table, letting the other people around it size me up as looking for an autograph, then said, "Mr. Louis ... , " at which he looked quickly at me and nodded slightly.

"Would you mind giving me an autograph?" I asked, stuttering a little.

He nodded, and I reached inside my suit's breast-pocket for a pen. He seemed to flinch when I reached into the jacket, and he watched me carefully while I tried to find, in the same pocket, a piece of paper that could be autographed. All I could come up with was the receipt for my hotel bills, which I would need to get those monstrous expenses reimbursed, and the hangers-on were looking less amused by the second. So finally I took the receipt, and handed it to Louis for him to sign the blank side for me. He looked at me till I handed him the pen as well, then scribbled his name quickly but legibly, and politely handed it back.

"Thanks very much, I really appreciate it," I said, then turned and walked back to Stella, avoiding any look toward Ed Sullivan. I knew that when we went back upstairs I would catch hell for not getting Sullivan's autograph, and I ought to have taken the same piece of paper over and asked for him to sign it too, but I was pretty flustered.

31

Close Encounters

So that was the first time in Las Vegas for me, and no poems came of it; the second time, in 1978 or so, I had to write about it, the result being "Close Encounters." That poem has been printed in *An Eagle Nation*. It rose up like smoke out of the abyss between two kinds of traditional Indian stories: the printed texts and translations of Osage ceremonies on the one hand, and the bawdy Trickster Tales (both Indian and other) on the other—both of which I was reading for certain courses I was teaching in 1973–74. What gave it more than cloudy presence was the stories of my Ponca cousins, when I went in to see them during the occupation of Wounded Knee, and afterwards as I would talk with them on the phone or go down to White Eagle for time with Ponca folks there.

Inside Wounded Knee, for instance, I was as always amazed at how my cousins could laugh and joke as they welcomed me to the "free Oglala Nation," how strong and humorous the Indian people I met there were. There had been heavy firing from the ring of surrounding U.S. troops, and from the anti-AIM "short-hairs" out-side, into the places where the occupying Indians were sleeping and eating, and the food was very low. But two things seemed crucial to me about what was happening in there. The first was that there were traditional medicine people and elders inside who were giving help and guidance, and there had lately been ceremonies held, of which my cousin Carter spoke with great seriousness. The second was that the morale was high and jokes were being made as always. I was reminded in certain ways of how the British people described life in the London bomb shelters during Hitler's bombing in 1941. My cousin Dwain, who was in charge of the "housing detail," when I was first taken along to see him had just been putting up blankets and sheets to divide parts of the trading post (I think it was) into "private rooms" for individuals and families.

"Hey, Mike," he said, "sure good to see you, but we got to stop meeting this way. How come you only come to see me when somebody's about to shoot us? Last time I saw you it was when that redneck in Oklahoma in 1953 was gonna beat you to a pulp, and me and Jim had to get the tire iron out of the car to stop him and then his buddy pulled a pistol out of the glove compartment. Now here we are having to duck the tracer bullets so we can talk about the good old days."

A month or so later, I learned that Dwain had been captured trying to slip out of Wounded Knee through the besiegers, but after being processed and jailed briefly he was let go because there was nothing to charge him with except being in the vicinity with a shotgun and rifle. I heard this from his mom, Aunt Jewell, who was then living out in Los Angeles, and she gave me the phone number where I could reach him for any further information about the situation of occupants in Wounded Knee when he left—my other cousins still being inside, and their telephone having been cut off. So I phoned him.

"Hey Mike," he said, "glad I can talk to you without machine guns pointing at me for once."

"Well, what the hell you doing outside, Bucky?" I asked.

"Tell the truth, Mike, I blew my mission," he said. "We realized it was getting near the end, the food was not going to hold out and they had tightened up so not enough was likely to get through again. So Carter and the other leaders decided we would try to get some of the guns belonging to the local people out of there. We realized that all the weapons would be confiscated and mostly all we had was the shotguns and rifles that the local Indian people had for hunting and brought in with them. They gave me and some other guys a few and we tried to get out with them after midnight one night when it was snowing and real cold. The last people to get in with food told us where to try and get through the lines.

Unfortunately those 82nd Airborne guys had got a lot of high-tech stuff in there to spot us at night. We knew they had sensors that would detect anybody moving from about knee-high on up, but we thought we could stay under their sensor-levels. We did okay crawling for a good while and then when I was trying to slip along the edge of a rockface it was real icy and I slipped down over it trying to hang onto the guns and made a noise. But the really bad thing was that as I tumbled down over those icy rocks I hit kind of awkwardly and busted my balls and let out a yell. Next thing I knew a big Airborne man in camouflage outfit had his boot in my face and his gun jammed in my chest and that was all she wrote."

So, what I was hearing was Coyote stories, how Trickster failed to trick the tough guys again. I kept thinking about Indian ceremonies, Indian humor, about the gambling and the ability to accept defeat and come back for another try. A friend, Jules Zanger, asked me about that time to come and speak informally to an American Cultural Studies group just across the Mississippi from where I teach, and I chose to speak about the kind of trickster stuff we can see in the antics of Huckleberry Finn on the one hand, and those of the Indians inside Wounded Knee on the other. And not long after that, there was going to be an annual meeting of the Rocky Mountain Modern Language Association, which would be held in Las Vegas, and I decided to work on that talk and make it a scholarly paper. It was accepted for presentation, which got my travel paid to and from Las Vegas to give it, and I stayed over three nights there—not in the Sands and Stardust Inn where the main convention sessions were held and most people stayed, but in a less expensive and far less crowded and noisy Travelodge a half-mile or so down the road.

I never did publish the paper, but for a long time afterwards, I kept thinking about the way the old ceremonies and the new bawdy resistance seemed to go together in Indian country. Then it occurred to me that I had written, a few years before, and published in a special issue of a journal which Roberta Hill Whiteman was editing, a short poem which was all and only about the Osage ceremonies, and I decided it needed to have the other side of what Gerald Vizenor calls "survivance" added to it—the Trickster side, the funny side, the kind of all-out willingness to take the low road if it might get us home. So I got out the poem and started working it over. The result was "Close Encounters"—the title of course related to that movie, *Close Encounters of the Third Kind.*

Close Encounters

I.

We of the Osage Nation have come,
as the Naming Ceremony says,
down from the stars.
We sent ahead
our messengers to learn
how to make our bodies,
to make ourselves a nation,
find power to live, to go on,
to move as the sun rises and never fails
to cross the sky into the west
and go down in beauty into the night,
joining the stars once more
to move serenely across the skies
and rise again at dawn, letting
the two great shafts of light beside the sun
become white eagle plumes in the hair
of children as we give their names.

When we came down, our messengers
encountered beings
who let us take their bodies
with which we live into the peaceful days.
We met the Thunder, and the Mountain Lion,
the Red Bird, and the Cedar Tree,
Black Bear, and Golden Eagle.
As eagles, we came down,
and on the red oak tops

we rested, shaking loose with our weight
great showers of acorns, seeds
for new oaks, and our daily bread.

The leaves were light and dancing and
we saw, through the trees,
the sun caught
among leaves moving
around its light. It was
the leaves, we saw,
those light beings, who raised
as they danced the heavy
oak-trunks out of earth,
who gathered the wind and sunlight,
the dew and morning into timbered
lodges for the sun and stars.

And so, of course, we sang.
Nothing's lighter than leaves, we sang,
ghost-dancing on the oak tree as the spirit moves,
and nothing heavier than the great
sun-wombing red oak which their dancing
in time has raised up from this earth where we
came down as eagles.
It will not end, we sang,
in time our leaves of paper will
be dancing lightly, making a nation of
the sun and other stars.

2.

Coming down to Las Vegas as
a passenger on Frontier Airlines is
a myth of another color. At the Stardust Inn, deep
within that city of dice and vice and Warhead Testing,
I was to give a paper
to the Rocky Mountain Modern Language Association
on Trickster Tales.

I gave it, and
I got out solvent, astonished,
and all but stellified
on wings of flame—like Elijah
or Geoffrey Chaucer in the *House of Fame,* up
up into the stars above Lake Mead, and I looked down
into the lake's twinkling heaven
and thought back to the many-splendored
neon and krypton lights of Las Vegas
that throbbed with the great lake's power.
I remembered the dead rapids and waterfalls
drowned in Glen Canyon and Lake Mead,
thought of those bodies of
water swollen so huge that earth itself
quivers with constant
small tremors from them—
and there, looking up at me with his
Las Vegas eyeball, was the Trickster Monster,
flashing with lightning from his
serpents of copper lifted up on crossbars—
but then I remembered how
among the streaked and painted bluffs that surround
Las Vegas I saw the October dawn come streaked
and painted down from the eastern skies to brighten
the walk from my Travelodge over the street
to a vacant lot under
its desert willows
where lived a wren, some vivid orange flowers
papery on thornleaved stems hugging the sand,
and one empty billfold
with its credit cards spread around a sole
identity card that pictured
a security guard from San Diego,
that naval base there.
I turned the billfold in
to the motel clerk, the wren
pleaded innocent and flew away like me,

and when I got the orange flower
back to St. Louis and put it into
a glass of water, it turned that water
to pungent amber then wilted as if
I'd killed it with kindness.
—That Trickster, he always carries
lost identity cards and desert flowers,
and finds himself
surrounded by dawn.

And so I sang
how the white sails of Columbus, of
Cortez and the Pilgrims, brought
this krypton iris here and made
the desert bloom,
how they raised
the great light-sculptured houses
of cards and dice on sand—
I sang how
the rainbow ghosts of waterfalls
are pulsed into the sockets of
Las Vegas lights and flash in crimson, green,
gold and violet its humongous word,
VACANCY
VACANCY
up to
the dancing stars.

32

Indian Survival, Four
At Cahokia Mounds

That poem, "Close Encounters," is more gnarly in its language,
more bristlecone than balsam fir, more professorial than I'd like.
Sometimes I try to tell stories more plainly, talk more naturally. One
of these came from a powwow held over at Cahokia Mounds for
which my Ponca Aunt Jewell, who was then eighty years old, was
named the Princess and came up for the occasion to dance, bringing
her daughter Casey to dance for her some of the time. Usually, of
course, a Powwow Princess is a younger woman, often beautiful in
face and body but always chosen as someone who is respected for
living in good Indian ways. But those who were putting on the
Cahokia Powwow wanted to show, on this occasion, how much they
valued and respected the Indian elders, how important the older
people are to our survival and to making our survival a good one.
Evelyne Wahkinney Voelker and her family, Comanches from
Oklahoma, were among those who named Aunt Jewell as Cahokia
Princess, and they saw to it that she was treated like a Princess when
she came and danced. Aunt Jewell and two of her grandchildren,
Mayke and Amelia, were asked to stay in the house of Margaret
Brown—who is the caretaker at Cahokia Mounds State Park, where
there are many mounds remaining from the time (about A.D. 1000–
1400) when this was the largest city north of the great metropolises
of Mexico.

The park is sited just across from St. Louis, where the Missouri River joins the Mississippi from the west, the Illinois from the northeast—and not far upstream from where the Ohio also joins that great river of rivers as it flows southward from Cahokia. Along all those rivers, the traders of the Mississippian Culture, the Mound Builders, flourished for more than a thousand years, and brought down copper from the Great Lakes, dentalium shells from the Pacific, other items from the Gulf of Mexico or the mountains of Appalachia. It was a great Confluence of Waters, the St. Louis and Cahokia area, and in the palisadoed city-state of Cahokia there were great mounds and plazas, wood-henges of tall cedar poles aligned so that the people could mark the seasons and forecast the lunar and solar and planetary movements to time their ceremonies. An Illinois state park now centers there, and a museum with its gift shop and restaurant and parking lot provides a good education to those who come to learn. The largest of the mounds, what is called "Monks' Mound" (because in the nineteenth century a monastic order held that to itself), has more volume than the Great Pyramid of Egypt though it is not as high. Wooden railroad ties have been placed as steps for tourists to climb up the mound, and from its top they can look west across the Mississippi at the glinting stainless steel Gateway Arch set there as a monument to the Westward Expansion of America after the Louisiana Purchase in 1803. It is what is called a catenary arch, rising six hundred and thirty feet over the riverfront like a giant croquet wicket. Underground between its legs and around it is another museum, the Jefferson Memorial one; the arch's legs are hollow and an elevator takes visitors up for a brief look out the heavy windows set into the top of the arch at the Mississippi roiling below it, across toward Cahokia to the east, and back toward St. Louis and California to the west.

In the late 1970s our St. Louis Indian Center had debated whether it might be all right to hold a powwow on the Cahokia grounds, the worry being that there are a great many bodies buried under some of those mounds, not all of which have been excavated. After a lot of thought and conferring, it was decided that with prayers and ceremonies we could ask the Old People there to let us do this, and afterwards the Parks people cooperated with our local

Indian community people and began holding a three-day festival, with powwow dancing, in late September of each year. Our St. Louis Powwow—of the American Indian Center of Mid-America, that is—is held in early September, the weekend nearest the first full moon that month, and the Cahokia Powwow about two weeks later.

So that's the context of the 1995 Cahokia Powwow at which my Ponca Aunt Jewell was named Powwow Princess. She and quite a few of her family had just come up to our St. Louis Powwow two weeks before, and Aunt Jewell—with her titanium knee and nitro-glycerine heart, her quick wit and beautiful laughter and fierce wisdom—had danced at that too, along with her daughter Casey, Casey's children Suzeta, Julie, Jeff, and of course Mayke and Amelia. There is always the question, when a large contingent of family has to make this five-hundred-mile drive from White Eagle and Red Rock, of what cars may be alive and chugging. Indians have a term, "powwow car," for the kind of beatup but still driveable old car, preferably a big roomy one and fairly soft-sprung, that people can drive all day and night while some are sleeping, to get over the great distances from home to the powwow and back. Luckily, that September, a usable powwow car had turned up, and Aunt Jewell and family had come rolling in fairly well rested, driving a big old Ford LTD. I did not ask how they came up with it.

At the Cahokia Powwow I took part in the Gourd Dancing and, as a Gourd Dancer, in the Grand Entry and all. But mostly I got to sit next to my aunt, the Powwow Princess, sitting there in her beautiful outfit with that crown on her head, and be happy talking with her. Something happened, though, that worried me a lot, and I mentioned it to her as we were sitting there: I saw my Uncle Gus— Aunt Jewell's brother—dancing over to the north side of the drum, and Uncle Gus had passed on over twenty years before. He had been the greatest of Ponca dancers, having won the first ever World Championship Fancy Wardance at the Haskell dances in 1926 or so, and had been recognized as one of the best ever, all through the 1920s and 1930s, before he got older, and the great Comanche dancer Woojie Watchataker came along and began to win the contests Uncle Gus had been winning.

When I told Aunt Jewell that I had just seen Uncle Gus out

there, she did not say anything for a few minutes, just nodded. At
the right time, she began talking to me of having gone up the month
before to the Sun Dances on the Rosebud Sioux Reservation in
South Dakota, and I thought she was changing the subject and did
not want to speak of Uncle Gus being there, maybe because that
could mean some one of our elders might be passing soon, or maybe
just because as his sister, and much older than he lived to be, she
was not eager to speak of him at this dance.

My ignorance and maybe my fear was making me misunder-
stand. She was telling me about what I had seen, and telling me it
would be taken care of. At the Sun Dances, she was saying, where
she had lately been, such things were known to happen, and there
were ways the elders had of taking care of them. And then she said
something unexpected to me: "Listen to that song," she said. My
hearing aids are always less helpful than natural ears, particularly in
the boom and buzz of public address systems at a powwow, amid all
the talk and bustle of the sidelines and the flash and shuffle and
twirl of dancers around the drum. So when I listened, at first I
heard only indistinct vocables and a song which I did not quite recognize though it was familiar. I first thought the word that emerged
from the fog of sound was *kah-geh*, "brother," but Aunt Jewell
shook her head and said emphatically, "*Listen* to that song!" and
then I heard: the Drum were singing the honor song of Uncle Gus
himself, and were calling his name, *Shon-geh-ska*, "White Horse."

Maybe the point is still not as clear as it should be, though an
Indian audience would not need to have it spelled out. Neither of us
had said anything to the Drum, and this song was not part of the
program that the emcee had lately told us would be going on just
now. But when I heard Uncle Gus's name, I realized that just before
this song had begun, one of the singers, Earl Fenner, had stood up
at the drum and come back to the emcee and spoken quietly to him
before going back out to sit down, and I now understood that Earl
had for some reason called this song for Uncle Gus, and had gone to
let the emcee know. I never asked anyone how it came about that
just after I saw Uncle Gus dancing there, a singer had decided to
call this song and start it. Aunt Jewell never tried to explain it
either; she was content once I heard that they had called the song,

and she left it to me to understand what was going on. There were other things that night that, by the next morning, I realized were part of the story as well. So the next morning I got up early, and wrote this story into a kind of poem, and before Aunt Jewell and family went home from the powwow that afternoon I gave it to them. In 1999 it was published in the journal *Flyway*.

Aunt Jewell as Powwow Princess

I was AGHAST at what I saw,
      I've got no way of seeing things like that.
           Felt kind of like I was sitting on a rock
   and suddenly I saw a label on it
            that said, URANIUM.
     Sometimes it's super-real, you see into things,
         I mean you see
     what isn't there, but yet it makes
   the things you CAN see have a different meaning.
              I think for some Indian people just
       like for physicists who figure how
          to look inside some distant star, it's possible
      to see how each thing, deep inside,
is something else, all made of crazy things
           they may give crazy names,
        quarks or whatever they may choose.
               Well hell, for instance right
       here in that word "aghast" which I just used, there lives
    a "ghost"—because one thousand years ago, inside
      those Anglo-Saxon warriors, the soul
    that spoke and danced, they didn't call that
   a SPIRIT but a GAST—so when they said AGHAST,
   they meant something was walking in their SOUL.
   So after all, maybe it's just as good to say
   "Ghost Dance," as "Spirit Dance," the way
        Americans say it, speaking
      of what the people did who are called,
       because of Columbus, INDIANS. Maybe

inside this English word INDIAN
there is a GHOST that haunts
all English-speakers, even in these words.

But here's the story: across the Mississippi from St. Louis,
there at Cahokia Mounds—
where we were dancing for
that Powwow-time
with Evelyne and her Comanche family,
who now are with Aunt Jewell and
our Ponca family as
an Eagle Nation, gathered by the passing
within their tepee of the Pipe among us—I sat one night
on a folding chair as Bob and Evelyne's sons
were dancing the Eagle Dance, and heard
Aunt Jewell tell me a story, that
September of her eighty-first year, of what she'd seen
under the first full moon
in August at a Sun Dance on the Rosebud. She said
they'd put the pole up in the night
under a huge moon, and then
the elders warned them, while the dancers there
were coming out in the Spirit Light to dance, of what
they might be seeing, and how
to understand, be calm, to hear
the strong-heart cries of warriors and
to know there were so many
of the Old People who would want
to come into the circle and dance, but now
they would be taken care of.
And then she heard their cries and saw
among the shadowy dancers spinning there
so many others just outside the arbor crowding in
long lines from where
the moon had risen—but they WERE
all right, she could see, without exactly
SEEING—

inside, she KNEW. I listened
to what she said, and at first
I only thought she was saying
how powerful the Sun Dance is, but then I saw—
I remembered how that afternoon
Earl Fenner came out from the drum and spoke
with our emcee Dale Besse, then went back
and started a song, and
Aunt Jewell said, LISTEN, and I said I heard
them singing KAH-GEH, "brother," and I looked at her
but she said firmly LISTEN to the WORDS,
and finally I heard: SHON-GEH-SKAH,
White Horse, Uncle Gus's name, they sang.
So then I understood
why she was telling about the Sun Dance, it was because
that afternoon she'd seen—without my saying anything—
that I was worried because I had just seen,
myself, under the half-moon in the daylight skies
there at Cahokia where the great city
of Indian people once had been,
her brother dancing, Uncle Gus,
who left us twenty years before,
and I don't see such things, but I saw him there
twice, dancing with
the hawk's wing he carried—
and now this evening, when the lights were on
and a half-moon golden in the west
above what might become
a thunderstorm, she told me, "Sonny,
this year after we were at Crow Dog's
we went to another Sun Dance too. I want to tell you
just a little about it,
we want to watch these
Eagle Dancers now, but soon
we'll find a time and talk about it,
and you can write it down."
So I remembered, then, how calm

Uncle Gus's face was when he danced,
there on the north side of our circle, how still
and fierce with understanding,
the way he always was.
And I felt good.
They'd brought us in,
that afternoon,
for the first Gourd Dance,
the women with green willow branches, behind
the Eagle Staff the Voelkers made for our Center,
and it felt good. And after supper
hundreds of Harley Davidsons came rumbling in,
great burly bearded bikers, some with skulls
on the gleaming quiet thunder of their machines,
and women bikers, some straight up cool
and distant, others grinning
with license plates like SASI-1—
and one of our Board Members, Charlotte Pipestem,
Otoe and ex-Marine, rode in on the pillion
behind a huge man—all the bikers
were packing bags and boxes
of groceries and supplies
to give the American Indian
Center of Mid-America for
our Food Pantry where the people
are given food and things when they come in—
maybe five hundred Harley Davidsons, mostly
with two people on them, men, women and little kids,
they turned in off the highway
and rode around the arbor set up and covered
with its green willow branches in
a great circle under those ancient mounds,
the bikers came in on their beautiful machines
the way the warriors used to ride
their horses in,
and at the East where the dancers
would bring the Eagle Staff in, Evelyne

and the Head Singer, her brother Rusty,
   and the Head Man Dancer Warren Sovo, and
  a lot of us, Gourd Dancers, one ex-Ranger, took
with thanks the food those bikers brought, set
the plastic and paper bags and boxes down
in a great overflowing heap beside the Arbor,
  and rumbled off, I thought
    into the wild
      American yonder,
 and that felt good, we saw for now
    there's food for the elders and for
  the children, for all the people, what they have
   will be a feast—
 and I thought,
   well, now that's done, but it wasn't,
 then Rusty and the singers and the dancers
    called those bikers back into the Circle
   and they came
  on foot, over four hundred strong, and stood
   around the Drum
    while the Singers sang
 an Honor Song for them,
    and we dancers stood
   behind them in the Circle,
all the spectators stood, and the song was sung,
   and I did not see
  Uncle Gus again that evening as the moon
    was being covered by new clouds—
 which after the Closing Song when the Staff
   was posted sent a few small drops,
 and on the way home, after
    we'd passed beside the Arch,
 just as we turned onto Delmar for home,
  briefly
   came down as a heavy rain.

33

Indian Survival, Five
In the Solutrean Caves

Speaking of how Indian people survive as Indians, I wonder how long humans have been finding ways to recognize themselves in their animal beings. "Skins as Old Testament" looks at the prehistoric choices of identity and its transformations among the early hominids and down to the early Sapiens. Looking at the photos of cave-paintings from over twenty thousand years ago, I could see those bear skulls, rhinoceros and horse paintings as ways of getting back and forth between selves and not-selves, Us and Others. Even before the cave paintings and carefully arranged bones and candles, there was the moment when first a human put on that alien skin— and had to negotiate identities with it. The act of self-consciousness must have begun not only by seeing oneself in water, with the sky and the trees and the clouds strangely wrapped around our bodies to keep us alive in this strange new place, but by seeing ourselves in the skins of those other beings whose flesh gave us life. I see this as like the moment between Old and New Testament, and also between the whole Bible and all the before and after of human history which makes that book look so small and different the way an acorn looks small and different next to its oak on the one hand and a geode on the other. Acorn into oak, deer into human, older self into newer one, old religion recast as new one.

Skins as Old Testament

Wonder who first slid in
                    to use another creature's skin
    for staying warm—blood-smeared
                    heresy almost, Hunter becoming
Deer, Shepherd the Lamb as in flamelit
                    Dordogne caves or dim cathedrals—
        crawling inside the deer's
                            still-vivid presence there
    to take their lives from what had moved
                    within, to eat delicious life
            then spread its likeness over a sleeping
        and breathing self, musk-wrapped
                                inside the wind,
                    the rain,
                the sleet—
        to roll up in a seal-skin self beneath
                    a mammoth heaven
            on which the sleet would rap and tap,
        to feel both feet
                        grow warm even on ice
                        or in the snow—hand-chalicing
    new tallow flame as spirit
                        of passing life
            and every time a tingling
    revelation when the life
                came back into a freezing hand or foot
            after the fur embraced its flesh, still deeper
when human bodies coupling in
        a bear's dark fur
                found winter's warmth and then
        its child
            within the woman
                came alive.

34

Indian Survival, Six
Among the Stars

Speaking of alien beings: when Richmond Lattimore, the fine translator of Greek plays and epics, came to dinner at our house, we had
a lovely polite Siamese cat, a seal point, whom Stella had named
Sappho. Just as we were seated ready to begin eating, Sappho looked
in. She was, I think, trapped in a part of the house where she had
fled when the visitor arrived, and being shy, she wanted but was
reluctant to cross the room to her own region of the house. Seeing
her in the doorway I thoughtlessly hailed her, "Oh, Sappho!"
Lattimore looked first somewhat unamused, though when Stella and
I laughed the frost melted and no one was ever more gracious to a
Muse's favorite. He spoke to her in Greek, to which she responded
with polite and soundless Siamese.

As a eulogy for Sappho, this may hint that earthlings might
deserve good treatment from any aliens who get here before we are
technologically equal to them. If the aliens are feline, and this poem
is meowable, perhaps it will help.

On the Planet of Blue-Eyed Cats

for Stella

Some moons of Jupiter are
as big as Earth almost;
its golden ones are sulphur, its

blue-and-white one ice—
Europa, Io, Ganymede, those old
love-victims of descending Zeus remembered in
their heavenly bodies—and now we
are sending Voyagers to be voyeurs
and catch them in the act
of eruption televised
to Pasadena, where the scientists cheer.
Their children will be flying out to Jupiter themselves,
in Solar Clipper ships may sail
on Mylar wings beyond the baths
of all the western stars,
their wind the sunlight and the sun's enormous
gravity to swing and glide against as red-
tailed hawks may ride updrafts for hours
then drop down on their prey;
but these will sail heavy-bellied back not
with bloody rabbits like the red-tailed hawks,
nor tea like clipper ships from China,
but rocks, brain-food for the
scientists, small pieces of the same old stuff,
but histories different from ours,
alterities to probe identities, the jargon goes.
Sliced up with diamond saws,
roasted in X-ray ovens, they will tell
us when their birthday was, just when
they joined the dancing satellites around
the satellites around the sun and through the
other stars; tell us just where we are
and how we came and where we voyage to.
It takes two things to be;
two places make a where;
two planets make a why.
So what are children for? Geoffrey,
Vanessa, Lawrence, would you please
go out to our back yard, and where your mother
has buried Sappho Prettypaws, who was older

than two of you and had a different history, would you set
a piece of the third planet out from our sun? And if
you hold it up first next to
a star, compare it even to Jupiter with all
those moons, it will not sparkle, but
it gives light back, our back yard's on
a blue star in its heaven—
and if
the little green star-people should come down
to check earth out before your children sail
out through their stars, you can
report to them that here a cautious blue-eyed
cat once walked upon and is a part
of earth which they have come to take. Maybe
you can tell by looking at them
how much they follow what you've said to them.
There is so much to understand in even
the simplest human acts,
even the simplest human love, say
of that shy kitten your mother raised,
her wordless judgment of our acts,
her choosing over and over
your mother as beloved,
as trustworthy, when Sappho
was having kittens and she knew
your mother was there for her, and she let
her fondle them and purred, knowing and trusting
this was her friend.
And if those little
green persons understand, even just
a part of what you've said, why then you'll have
a thoughtful friend among the starry powers,
maybe someone for whom
the earth is not a source
of wealth, of slaves, of power, but is
a place where mothers keep alive

what all such voyagers come to find,
wherever wandering matter gives them place
and time and mind to live,
to move, to learn a little of
what beings mean.

35

Discovering America
Antelope Canyon

In the high searing desert of the Navajo Reservation just south of
the Grand Canyon, one of the watercourses that have been carved
into the stone is called Antelope Canyon. One stretch of this is a
chasm cut into the sandstone, deep and sheer, with a narrow twist-
ing bottom, ordinarily dry, which can be hiked and is a favorite place
for tourists, who pay local guides to lead them down and along its
course, not far above where it runs into Lake Powell, the enormous
dammed-up lake which fills that part of the Grand Canyon.

In early August of 1997, a guide was leading eleven European
tourists along the bottom of Antelope Canyon, while other tourists
were walking high above on the canyon's rim, able to see down to its
bottom and to hear the hikers down there. But it happened that on
this occasion, at the top of the watershed many miles upstream, a
great thunderstorm broke, and its heavy downpour came rushing
down Antelope Canyon in a wall of water which trapped and over-
whelmed the hikers, sweeping them down amid mud and sand and
rocks and small boulders toward Lake Powell. The tourists up on
the canyon rim, unable to help, could hear everything as it happened.
All those below, except for the guide, who managed to scramble up
above the onrushing water, were drowned.

Indian Country
That Dark Romantic Chasm

They came from England, Sweden, France, "America"—
    alive and earnest,
        wanting to see America,
            see where the Indians live in
        the desert and the high clear air,
            wanted to go down into
        the rocky spiritual chasm and look up where
            red sandstone parted for
        an azure heaven to come down,
    and it came down,
        but far upstream it fell,
            the black thundering clouds poured down
        their pent-up rainbows into stone channels,
            the beating heart of storm pulsed
        its waters down Antelope Canyon and over
            the pilgrims while their Eurekas
    went echoing up to those standing untouched
        and dry on the canyon's rim, hearing, hearing
    how their helpless bones were hurled
        down the swift hammering stream to the lake,
    the great tranquil lake, deep in the Grand Canyon
        where slowly, slowly,
    they may be found again,
            and taken up and out of
        the stone and back
    to Europe where those
            who loved them wait
    to mourn and lay them under
        a gentle earth,
            with flowers,
                yet once more.

36

Soul and Body Medicine

By the 1980s, herbal medicines had got to be quite a business in the United States. So many people had experience of the way "modern medical miracles" not only failed to cure but seemed to make them sicker than the sickness itself—chemotherapy for cancers, for instance—that desperate remedies were being sought. The discovery that extract from a particular yew-tree's bark could shrink certain tumors seemed another bit of evidence that "folk medicine" or even "old Indian herb-doctors" might have cures which medical technology had missed, or drug companies in search of profits were not studying.

Not only "bodily" but "spiritual" ailments, among the considerable number of people who view our profit-driven and technology-dominated society as self-poisoning, urgently need remedies. Here also, "Indian" ways were examined for "spiritual cures"—whether by sweatlodge and pipe and peyote ceremonies, or by homilies of Wise Elders, or by the laying on of hands (so to speak) of Young Writers. Not only "New Agers" in the United States, but romanticizing "Indian lovers" from European countries set up whole "tribes," put on paint and feathers and chanted and "went native." Besides such cultists, however, there were a good many sensible people who looked for practical herbal medicines for colds, for flus, for various kinds of illness that they considered both bodily and spiritual in nature.

One of the plants whose roots had long been known to be useful in these ways is the "purple coneflower" or "snakeroot," source

of echinacea which grows well in the Tallgrass Prairie country of
the Osage Reservation, especially in the Buck Creek Valley's meadows
where I was raised. Echinacea is considered to strengthen the immune
system, and thereby help the body to throw off colds and flus and
other ailments. In the 1980s, my Osage folks (my stepfather Addison,
and his grandsons David and Denver and Danny especially) found
that they could dig this "snakeroot" and sell it to dealers for a fair
amount of money—though nothing like the amounts which the
dealers got from the national and international producers of the
extract. So it hit me one day that this was a situation in which the
"spiritual" values of Indians and "others" could be figured quite
clearly, and that meant a poem was waiting to find words. Here are
the words I found. I should add that in the second part of this, the
"Cakes" part, I refer to a cookbook author as "Erma Bombauer,"
which was in the beginning my mistake for "Irma Rombauer," but I
have left it that way because I like the combination of Erma Bombeck
and the author of *The Joy of Cooking*, especially since the whole
passage is tongue in cheek (wordplay intended).

Spirituality 101
Snakeroot

Used to pick the dead coneflowers,
                    after their drooping purplish petals
        had fallen off and the heads
                stood nodding over November bluestem where
                    sometimes a meadowlark might seem
        to take an interest in their bristly-seeded centers—
                so easy, walking, to put a hand down and
            run forked fingers up along the rough stem
                    and pull a head off, crumble and toss
        the seeds as I walked—
                    helping, I guess, field mice
            a little bit, maybe getting a few
                    into the ground to keep
            the meadow full of them.
Sixty years later, in our suburban

back yard they grow, planted
　　by my Edenic wife who says I must have done
before she met me
all the gardening I was ever going to do, because
　　I never dig, or plant, or trim, or weed—
　　　　I tell her Mother Nature's better at it
　　and I don't want to interfere—and you know,
I almost got away with that excuse, but didn't.
That's why she thought I was joking when
　　　　I told her these coneflowers
were medicine plants.
　　　　　　"No, seriously," I said,
　　I'll show you," and I got the book.
　　　　"See, *Echinacea,* that's the stuff."
She couldn't deny the pictures were just like it.
　　　　"Besides," I said,
"it's these they call *snakeroot,* these are what
　　　　my sister's boys are digging from our meadow
and selling roots and making a hundred dollars a day
from some middle-man in Bartlesville
　　　　who sells them to some foreign buyers.
They say those Europeans love this stuff.
　　All the herbal shops and organic people
　　swear by it now, they say it helps
　　　　　　the immune system—see,
　　even this book says so."
　　　　　　　　Of course
it's getting scarcer now in the wild, my nephews
　　　　told me last time I went to Oklahoma
　　they drive sometimes up into Kansas, even Wyoming,
　　　　　and out into the meadows there to dig,
　　but lately the big landowners there
　　　　　　came round and saw them digging
　　and sicked their men with guns on them
　　　　and ran them off, said
if they caught them there again

the best thing that might happen to them
would be hard time in jail, if they survived.
Aunt Jewell was hoping, though,
        that they might dig enough one June
and July to get a powwow car that might transport her
          up to the Sun Dance in July.
She told me, when I phoned,
David and Denver and her grandson Mikasi
    already took the pickup up
through Nebraska into South Dakota, said
        the snakeroot up there can be dug,
at least nobody'd chased them off, so far.
When I went over to talk and read some poems
        at Haskell Indian University there in Kansas,
I had a 'flu I couldn't seem to throw off,
    a heavy cough, but Denise
who teaches there made me some tea
    and said, "Here, put some of this in,"
took out a small bottle with eye-dropper lid,
    and dropped in several drops.
It had an astringent taste,
    was kind of bitter.
        The bottle's label said
some German company made the stuff.
    Cleared up my 'flu right away—maybe
placebo power, or it got more spiritual
    crossing the Atlantic twice.
So far as I know, none of the coneflowers here
    in our suburbs is ever used for medicine.

Spirituality 102
Cakes and Ale, Bread and Wine

"Do you have a cake in that oven?"

"Not yet."

"Then what is in there?"

"Well, we call it a cake because we don't have any other word in
    English for a cake in the baking stage. Tewas would maybe call
    it a Raw Cake."

"Could I look at it to see for myself? Maybe taste it?"

"No, that would probably spoil it."

"So you don't want me to know about your cakes and baking skills?"

"Well, have you got some flour, sugar, butter, water, vanilla extract,
    lemon juice, eggs, baking powder, maybe some crossed fingers
    and prayers, an oven you find trustworthy, something to whip
    with and a bowl with a big spoon. . . . don't you know how to
    make a cake yourself?"

"Not a spiritual cake."

"Oh. I guess you should go buy a cookbook."

"Which one has a spiritual recipe?"

"Erma Bombauer. She got it right from a frybread cook at White
    Eagle Oklahoma, knew my Aunt Jewell when she used to make
    cakes with commodity lard."

"Can I write a book about it?"

"Sure. And will you give me a piece, if it doesn't Fall?"

"Oh yes. I'll call it Bread of Heaven, and I'll feed you till you want
    no more."

"Many thanks, and the bookstore's thataway."

37

Foresight and Hindsight

Andrew Marvell saw surprising things in a drop of dew. A pool of water does not have to be very deep to hold a galaxy, or a flower, or many lives among its light and shadows. Just above the old pond our grandfather scooped out at the edge of our meadow, and just below the new pond a bulldozer dug and dammed, the little gully that carried the overflow from the new pond into the old one had a shallow pool, a foot and a half deep maybe, with the bluestem hay and its bright flowers nodding above and reflected on the pool's surface. There were persimmon trees growing around and above it too, and among these and the wild grapes, button-bushes, and berry-vines beneath them was where we used to dump our worn-out furniture, broken toys, rusty pots and pans, that we had used from the 1930s when we first moved out to Buck Creek to live. I always felt haunted by this place, which first taught me history, how things don't stay, how the ground takes them under and the grass goes over what was part of your life.

Even in a hot dry summer, that little pool would be there, and in the 1960s whenever I went back for a visit to my folks at Buck Creek I liked to walk down there, especially when the meadow was full of wildflowers, and look at the pool, so absolutely mirror-still and lucid down under its loamy bank. There sometimes were craw-dads moving slowly along its bottom, and water-striders walking over its surface, all of them seeming to move among the flowers reflected on the pool's surface, but also among the shadows of the water-striders that were cast down from the surface onto the bottom where the crawdads were grazing.

One day when I was standing and looking at this, I noticed that a water-strider's shadow made a kind of skull-image—two big shadow-eyes, a kind of shadow-nose, and a curious sort of shadow-mouth there. Then as I looked at this, the strider turned around and sprinted across the pool, and stopped with its shadow precisely beneath an image of white larkspur blossoms—but upside down, the "skull" now looked like a butterfly with wings outspread, and when it stopped right "on" that larkspur it was as if a butterfly with wings of shadow had stopped to taste a flower.

At that time I was putting together a collection of poems, and some of them made up a section that I called "Home Movies." These pieces were elegies, or eulogies, for my grandfather, three of my uncles, and my twin sister, who had died over the years from 1955 to 1971. I saw, looking into the pool of water, how to write a poem that would begin this set of family pieces—how the skull could become a butterfly, the surface sky and flowers live peaceably with the creatures beneath, how the shadow beings could taste again some sweetness, in words at least.

But I saw that only after I put the pool and its beings into words. At first I did not see or describe this as some version of human lives or reversals of fortune or spirits crowding like those called up by Odysseus who come forward out of their dark unhappy afterlife into the daylight for a little while and tell their stories. I described it as a pool on the meadow at Buck Creek where I lived. Only when I understood, having written the description, that it was as much about the lives of our family there as it was about the lives of the water and earth and air and their creatures in and around the pool, did I look for a title for the poem that might point the reader to join the two visions, of the pool and of our lives and times.

The title I found was a phrase from Hamlet's soliloquy (act 4, scene 4) when he is trying to get himself psyched up to act swiftly, once he gets back to Denmark, to revenge his father. Looking at a whole army going to fight another army for a worthless plot of ground too small to hold the graves of those who will be killed over it, Hamlet makes two things of the scene: first, it is a sign of mortal disease within the body politic, a kind of abscess which will kill the state when it breaks, an abscess caused (he says) by too much "wealth and peace." Yet he then views the scene as showing the true greatness of Prince Fortinbras, who is here "Exposing what is mortal and unsure / To all that fortune, death, and danger dare, / Even for an eggshell." Fortinbras, in this view, is showing what it is "rightly to be great," finding "quarrel in a straw / When honor's at the stake." So Hamlet concludes that he ought to take this as his model, since he has so much greater cause to take to the sword than Fortinbras does, and since God has given human beings the power of reason precisely so they will not spend their lives just sleeping and eating:

Sure he that made us with such large discourse,
Looking before and after, gave us not
That capability and godlike reason
To fust in us unused.

It is certainly one of the most muddled speeches by one of the most muddled characters Shakespeare ever put into words. But the phrase "looking before and after" is the one that interests me here. It was picked up, two hundred years later, by Shelley, and used with a rueful difference in his "To a Skylark," in the favorite stanza of Rumpole of the Bailey:

We look before and after,
And pine for what is not;
Our sincerest laughter
With some pain is fraught—
Our sweetest songs are those that tell of saddest thought.

This, I thought, was a phrase I could use as the title for a poem which looked into a pool where skulls became butterflies tasting the image of white larkspur flowers.

Looking Before and After

Under the new pond-dam
a trickle

· like a spring fills
old pools among
the button-bushes where you
step between rusting bedsprings
blackberry vines
persimmon trees & wild grape tangles and
where the matted grass gives
way to shining there is
footdeep water so clear that over
its brown silt bottom, haloes dazzle round the
shadows trailed by water-striders in
their spindly-crooked dimpling across its
springy surface so
each bright-edged darkness glides up to
and over brown crawdads bulldozing through
the mud-dust,
and see, one shadow-cluster is
a gliding skull whose two
great eyes stare above its
nose and three black teeth,
it wanders,
lunges, glides,
spins upside down and turns
to butterfly! that stops precisely underneath
an image of white larkspur nodding upon
the water's surface so it seems
that dimly there
among cruising crawdads a
butterfly of shadows tastes
sweet light again.

38

Indian Survival, Seven
After Sand Creek

I began this book with Coyote telling why he sings. I can end it with
a story from my Ponca folks about why we still are singing.

A Song That We Still Sing

On the way from Oklahoma up to the Sun Dance
at Crow Dog's Paradise on the Rosebud Sioux Reservation,
they'd stopped a few minutes,
my Ponca cousins from Oklahoma—
they were way out there by some kind
of ruins, on the August prairie,
some kind of fort it may
have been, they stopped
to eat a little, get out and
stretch their legs, the van
had got too little for
the kids and all.
And they were walking
not paying much attention and they heard
the singing and then Casey said,
Listen, that's Ponca singing.
Hear it? Where's it coming from?
They listened, and Mike said,

Sounds like it's over
inside those walls or whatever
they may be, over there.
    So they walked
through the dry short grass
    towards the raised earth walls
and up on them, and looked
inside that wide compound, and there
    was not a soul in sight.
That was a Wolf Song, Mike said.
    Yes, a Victory Song, Casey said.

When they told me later, we looked and
    decided that it was where the Cheyennes
and some of their allies had chased some troopers
    inside a fort and
        taunted them—

        after Sand Creek it was,
    that time the news got out of what
        had been done to Black Kettle and
        his people there beneath
that big American flag which they'd been given
    in token that this peaceful band
        was not to be attacked,
    and then at dawn the Reverend Colonel
Chivington and his men attacked and massacred
    some hundreds who could not escape—
        one small boy, running
    for refuge, was shot down at a hundred yards,
because, as Chivington had told his troops,
    Nits make lice. The women's breasts,
        sliced off, were made into
            tobacco pouches, as were the scrotums
of men. George Bent, a half-Cheyenne who was there,
            who'd been a Confederate soldier and
both wrote and spoke English and Cheyenne,

has told about it in his letters—
      he saw White Antelope come out
unarmed from his tepee, pointing up
at Old Glory waving over the village there,
      then when the troopers kept on shooting,
he stood unmoved and sang, as they shot him down,
      the death-song he'd composed for such a time:

        Nothing lives long
        except the earth and the mountains.

So I asked Casey and Mike,
      what do you think you heard, inside that place?
—*I guess,* Mike said, *up in Nebraska*
    there must have been some Poncas
      who joined the Cheyennes there and fought
    the soldiers till they chased them
        into that fort.
Then Casey said,
      We recognized that song. It's one
      that we still sing.

Notes

1. For more on riddles, see *Family Matters, Tribal Affairs* (176–83), and *American Indian Culture and Research Journal* 23.1 (1999): 177–89.

2. One poem I read in June 1994 was "Bringing in the Sheaves," and I mentioned having stayed in 1949 with the Parkers, whom I had not seen since then. After the reading, two people who had been sitting quietly at the very back of the room came up to speak with me, and I suddenly realized they were Mary Ellen and Calvin, who looked at least ten years older than they were in 1949. Right away Mary Ellen said she wanted to apologize for something she had done that summer. I said what in the world could that be, I remembered having a grand time in their place. "Well," she said, "when you and Walter left your suitcases in our house while you hitch-hiked down to Russell and Hays looking for jobs in the oil fields, while you were gone I went in to sweep and clean the room, and pulled your suitcase out from under the bed so I could sweep there."

At this point Mary Ellen blushed and stammered some. "The suitcase was really heavy," she said, "and I got just terribly curious about what in the world made it so heavy. So I am really ashamed to admit I opened it and looked, and found you had those books in there. I have wanted for over forty years to admit doing that and apologize to you." So I'd better send her and Calvin a copy of this book—which is considerably less heavy than Neilson's *Complete Works of Shakespeare*—to show I forgive them.

3. When, in high school, I read Shelley's "Ode to the West Wind," I thought Shelley had seen such a display:

Thou on whose stream, 'mid the steep sky's commotion,
Loose clouds like earth's decaying leaves are shed,
Shook from the tangled boughs of Heaven and Ocean,

Angels of rain and lightning: there are spread
On the blue surface of thine aëry surge,
Like the bright hair uplifted from the head

Of some fierce Mænad, even from the dim verge
Of the horizon to the zenith's height,
The locks of the approaching storm....

Later, at Oxford, the more pretentious English Lit people were
kowtowing to the Cambridge caco-critic F. R. Leavis, who in *Revaluation*
explained that Shelley was a bad poet because he had a weak grasp on
reality—an instance of which, said Leavis, could be seen in those lines
from "Ode to the West Wind." I can't blame Leavis for being provincially
ignorant about weather, but he was wrong in two arrogant assumptions:
first, that Shelley had not seen what he clearly described; second, that what
Leavis had not seen must not exist.

4. Frances Labadie, one of the original Osage Allottees, was at home
that day and watched as the storm came through and damaged the house
and buildings, but she and the others there survived. She was born in 1906,
just before the deadline for being put onto the roll of 2,229 Osages—the
roll that was drawn up that year so that the allotment of reservation lands
could be completed. To each enrolled Osage would go an equal share in all
income from leasing, mining or drilling and producing any subsurface
minerals on the reservation. Every one of these "headrights" turned out
to be worth, over the years from 1906 to 1929, hundreds of thousands of
dollars, because under the reservation was a pool of oil so large that several
oil companies grew great by successfully drilling for it—two that survive
today being Phillips 66 and Conoco.

I first met Frances Labadie, and reminisced with her about that 1942
tornado, almost sixty years later, in September 1999—when we both were
guests of the mayor of Montauban, in southwest France. The occasion was
the official signing of a document by which Pawhuska, Oklahoma, and
Montauban, France, became twin cities. Sitting next to Frances at the
table, I took a quiet moment during the feasting to ask if she remembered
the tornado of May 1942. Her eyes lit up: "SEE it? I was IN it!" she said,
and told me all the details. It was as though we were talking the very next
day after the tornado had passed.

As for the Montauban/Pawhuska *jumellage* ("twinning") in which we
were participating, thereby hangs a nineteenth-century tale—from the

years 1827–30, when a small group of Osage Indians were brought to
France as Noble Savages, to see and be seen by the French Nobility.
Lionized at first (introduced to King Charles X), the Osages were stranded
when the American army officer who had promoted the tour turned out to
be not only a French emigré, but a fugitive felon. After he was jailed in
Paris, the Osages wandered through Europe and then, hungry, tattered,
and penniless, back to France. They split into two small groups, and one
went north and was rescued by the aged Lafayette himself, who arranged
transportation back to America for them. The southern group had the
good fortune that Bishop DuBourg of Montauban heard of their plight.
Having himself been a priest in St. Louis who ministered to Osages before
returning to France and being elevated to a bishopric, DuBourg had the
Osages brought to Montauban, gave them full and gracious hospitality, and
raised the funds for their transportation back to America.

The Osages had kept this memory alive until 1989. In that year, the
mayor of Montauban, Jean-Claude Drouilhet, first read of the 1827–30
events in a French history journal. A man of extraordinary verve and
follow-through, he searched out the present location of the Osage Nation
in Oklahoma, and wrote (in French) to the mayor of the Osage Agency
town of Pawhuska there, proposing some kind of get-together to bring alive
again the warm relationship established a hundred and fifty years before
between the Osage and French people. The Pawhuska mayor at once con-
tacted the Osage chief and tribal council, and they found a tribal member
with an M.A. in French literature, Angela Robinson, to serve as translator
and letter-writer.

The result was that in 1991–92, and on other occasions since, a delegation of Osages and other Oklahomans traveled to Montauban, where the
red carpet was rolled out for them, and in turn considerable numbers of
people from Montauban came to Pawhuska (and Los Angeles, where many
Osages live) for equally festive hospitality. In mid-September 1999, it was
the turn of Montauban to host the Oklahoma delegation, and having heard
how splendid the food, the wine, the town, the region, and the people were,
I was hoping Stella and I might join the celebration. E-mails from the
generous hosts in Montauban told us to come ahead. As it happened, we
were to be in England for scholarly work during August, then I was booked
for a three-day poetry festival in Naples in early September, just as the
feasting in Montauban was to begin. So we flew from Naples to Barcelona,
rented a car, and drove up to Montauban for four terrific days. (I made
sure our route from Barcelona passed through Andorra, because I wanted

to look at that small "independent" country between France and Spain as one possible model for an American Indian nation.)

The *jumellage* of Pawhuska and Montauban is not merely sentimental. Jean-Claude Drouilhet has written a book in which he narrates the story of the Osages in France, 1827–30—but he sets that story into deep historical context, not only of Osage culture and history, but of the history and culture of the Languedoc region of France. This means that he brings out the parallels and analogies between the suppression and attempted destruction of Osage language, religion, and culture on the one hand, and the suppression and destruction of the Cathar religion, troubadour culture, and Occitan language by the Parisian central government and culture on the other hand.

But the *jumellage* is a business as well as a cultural matter: as with the "twinning" of cities in, say, England and Germany (Oxford and Bonn are "sister cities"), the effort is to foster ties of commerce as well as of culture. It did not seem to require many bottles of excellent local wine or many heaping plates of fish, fowl and meat, *fromages incroyables* and fruit irresistible, before our Oklahoma delegation saw the light on these matters. And there were "high-level" contacts to be made between the governor of Oklahoma and various French officials, in a meeting in Paris after the Montauban festivities, to see what business ties could be forged—including tourist interests, Indian crafts and writers, and (I hope) visits by French people to Oklahoma and elsewhere. Stella and I, however, left such treaty-making and fur-trading processes in good hands, and made our way back to St. Louis.

5. Part of what I learned from Professor Eikenberry, though, was learned while I was working, or just hanging around, in the English department, hearing him and the other teachers and graduate students talk—but the best part began in my sophomore year, when he called on me for assistance after he had suffered a severe eye-infection. For much of that year he was able to read only with one eye and for relatively brief periods. This meant not only that he could not read student papers as carefully, but could not spend his usual hours at night reading and re-reading the texts and secondary literature for his courses, making notes and preparing lectures and arranging seminar topics and discussions.

So I would walk over to his small flat on College Avenue several evenings a week, and read aloud the plays or other texts, and sometimes write down outlines and notes in a large hand for his lectures, and mark such passages from critics or journals as he found relevant to his courses.

He subscribed to *Partisan Review*, to the *Nation* and the *New Republic*, and to Cyril Connolly's British highbrow journal *Horizon* until it died about 1949; all those back issues were on his bookshelves, where I was allowed to read after he had gone to bed, until midnight if I wanted, and let myself out to walk back home. It was like having an Indian uncle to train me, but this time in the literary "wilderness."

He had let me, a sophomore, enroll on a trial basis in his Sixteenth Century seminar, and with all this "extra homework" I could make the grade alongside the five graduate and six seniors and special juniors. He picked me to read Shakespeare aloud while his sight was out, partly because he knew I was in dire need of money beyond what the scholarship and my hundred hours a month of English department and other duties paid me—but also because he knew from my freshman year's class-work, my keeping up with the seminar students, and departmental bull sessions, that I would do this job well.

I was already reading papers for an older freshman-comp teacher whose eyesight was failing—doing the preliminary red-pencil marking of spelling and grammatical mistakes for him, and referring students to grammar-book sections for each mistake. In junior and senior years I would do the preliminary paper-marking, and eventually much of the comment-writing, on Eikenberry's freshman composition papers. I had to ask now and then about fine details of syntax and word-nuances, and this led to a course in advanced English grammar that Professor Eikenberry taught for a small group of students, which together with the close reading of student compositions was a great way to learn how and why English sentences fancydance, gourd dance, or forty-nine. In my senior year I also took a course in History of the English Language from E. H. Criswell (then dean of Arts and Sciences), and saw how many sunken treasures await finding in the depths of the *Oxford English Dictionary;* and when later, at Oxford, I had to go scuba-diving into Grendel's mere with Beowulf, some of the maps I picked up in Oklahoma did mark the territory fairly well.

But what I have said here must leave the impression of all work and no play. One of the things I liked best about my favorite professors, Eikenberry and Hayden and Alworth, was that easy laughter moved with them—whether irising the mist of university "politics" or welling up fresh from a Shakespeare play.

There was, for instance, the night I found out why *The Two Gentlemen of Verona* is more than just readable. I was reading the play aloud to Professor Eikenberry while he prepared for his second day's lecture on the play. It was hard going, because I was reading it almost cold, having just

skimmed it for plot before his first lecture the day before. As I read aloud,
the serious parts came out as fussy and artificial, self-consciously stuffed
with wordplay ranging from the shallow obvious to the murky obscure.
I was too ignorant to catch most of the repartee, so my reading must have
been somewhat painful to a listener who knew it almost by heart. Sometimes I really could not figure how a sentence's cadences should fall, so he
would explain the nuanced joking which made sense of the passage, letting
it be read aloud with just the right intonation to keep strict meter *and*
render the meaning clearly. Now and then he would ask me to read a
speech again, and then would repeat some clause or sentence in a medita-
tive voice (never dramatic)—whereupon its meaning would dawn on me,
and I would say "Oh!" and re-read it, this time properly.

For all his guidance, though, I kept to my unspoken view that this was
pretty much a silly play. He understood that this was my view, just as
I understood that in his classroom lectures he was speaking as much to my
skepticism as to the usual dismissal of this play by critics. That night, as
I kept reading the play aloud, its artificial language began to seem easier,
clearer—almost, in fact, language that could have been really spoken by
very clever people to each other. It cleared up simply because it always had
a dramatic point, actually made sense. The people were really saying things
to each other, not just playing with words. This made them people, not
just poetic words on a page. I was beginning to read a Shakespeare play, to
realize this *was* a play.

But these real people—so I said to Professor Eikenberry that
evening—were still behaving like clever idiots, if not puppets. What they
said made sense, but what they did was senseless. Their falling in and out
of love, the betrayals of lover and friend and father and rival, were arbitrary,
sudden, human enough yet dramatically not believable. The plot was controlling the playwright. There was nothing comparable to what Shakespeare
invented in *A Midsummer Night's Dream*—that whole irrational rationale,
which boils down to those drops of love-juice that Puck squeezes into the
eyes of sleeping mortals and immortals, which make them fall wildly in
love with whatever they see when they wake. Without such a supernatural
excuse, the love-reversals in *Two Gentlemen* (I said) are not comic, they're
ridiculous.

Yet though the *Two Gentlemen* entirely lacked such an enchanting
world, I found—or, very subtly, was taught—something else that did
enchant me, something that only emerged as I read on into the second act.
Each of the play's "Two Gentlemen" has a servant—Valentine's is named
Speed, and Proteus's is named Launce. Speed comes on stage right away,

and has a lot of dialogue with Proteus in act 1 and with Valentine in act 2. His early lines I read with interest but not excitement, because his humor is all wordplay and paradox: he is smart enough to parody and satirize both the two Gentlemen, but he is never more than a standard comic servant, and the play's action stops while he bandies puns with one gentleman or the other.

Things change entirely when Launce appears for the first time in act 2, scene 3. His master Proteus is being sent off to the court of the Duke of Milan, and Launce has just learned that he must leave his family behind to accompany Proteus. He enters leading his dog Crab and talking in prose— and the voice comes right up off the page as natural speech. That's how I put it now: at the time, all I understood was that THIS speech was utterly hilarious and its speaker not at all "realistic" but entirely believable. What I did, in Professor Eikenberry's living room, was to fall apart laughing in the middle of Launce's fourth sentence. To show why, I'll have to quote those first four sentences:

> Nay, 'twill be this hour ere I have done weeping; all the kind of the Launces have this very fault. I have received my proportion, like the Prodigious Son, and am going with Sir Proteus to the imperial's court. I think Crab my dog be the sourest-natured dog that lives. My mother weeping, my father wailing, my sister crying, our maid howling, our cat wringing her hands, and all our house in a great perplexity, yet did not this cruel-hearted cur shed one tear.

The first sentence is marvelous because it brings before us from offstage the whole FAMILY scene that has just taken place. Launce has to be wiping his eyes as he comes onstage, I could see that—but what other playwright would have had a comic servant tell us that his whole family was tender-hearted like him, so that we know from just this second half of the first sentence where Launce comes from and what has been happening there? His second sentence tells us it is a Bible-reading family, wearing its piety as everyday dress—but Launce has got his pious breeches on back-wards, so to speak, not only in the unbuttoned verbiage of *prodigious* (not *prodigal*) *son* and *proportion* (not *portion*), but in the unintended implication that like the Prodigal Son, Launce is going out to waste his substance in riotous living.

So far, so funny, but fairly usual stuff. Now the *real* fun begins: he turns to his dog Crab and says, with sad solemnity, that he thinks Crab is the sourest-natured dog there is. And here, suddenly, that whole offstage scene is made to happen right before us: mother weeping, father wailing, sister crying, maid howling—and the last touch of genius, "our cat wringing her hands." It was right here that I collapsed in Professor Eikenberry's easy chair, while he sat over on the sofa and smiled, and chuckled a little, as I tried repeatedly to get back to reading the speech aloud, and every time I came to that cat wringing her hands, I had to give it up again and laugh till the tears came. Any sensible playwright would have stopped with that perfect final cadence: "yet did not this cruel-hearted cur shed one tear."

But no, that was only the beginning of Launce's monologue, which got crazier and funnier as it went along:

> Nay, I'll show you the manner of it. This shoe is my father; no, this left shoe is my father. No, no, this left shoe is my mother; nay, that cannot be so neither. Yes, it is so, it is so, it hath the worser sole. This shoe, with the hole in it, is my mother, and this my father; a vengeance on't, *there* 'tis! Now, sir, this staff is my sister—for, look you, she is as white as a lily, and as small as a wand. This hat is Nan, our maid. I am the dog. No, the dog is him*self,* and *I* am the dog! Oh—the dog is me, and I am myself: ay, so, so! Now come I to my father: "Father, your blessing." Now should not the shoe speak a word for weeping: now should I kiss my father: well, he weeps on. Now come I to my mother. O that she could speak like a wood woman! [Evidently the shoes were wooden; and wood still meant "raging mad," so Launce is solemnly wishing his wooden shoe could speak like a woman driven mad with grief.] Well, I kiss her—why, there 'tis, *here's* my mother's breath up and down! Now come I to my sister; mark the moan she makes. Now, the dog ... all this while, sheds not a tear, nor speaks a word; but see how I lay the dust with my tears.... (emphases added)

It was almost impossible for me to read the rest of act 2 after that. Luckily, it was only about eight in the evening, and my memory is that Professor Eikenberry went into the kitchen and brought out a quart of milk and a half-dozen glazed doughnuts, after which we got back to the play. By nine o'clock we had got over to act 4, scene 4, the last appearance of Launce in the play—once more with his dog Crab, whom Launce had disastrously tried to present as a gift from his master Proteus to the latter's new love, Silvia. Launce is sadly rebuking Crab for his misbehavior:

> Nay, I remember the trick you served me when I took my leave of Madam Silvia. Did not I bid thee still mark me, and do as I do?

> When didst thou see me heave up my leg, and make water against a
> gentlewoman's farthingale? Didst thou ever see *me* do such a trick?

At that point I fell apart again, and we had to postpone reading the rest of
the play to another evening.

The point of this, it will be recalled, is how the educating was done.
It was kind, tolerant, do-it-yourself but with the most expert guidance,
was both tutorial and classroom lectures. The teacher gave me far more
credit for understanding than I deserved, and therefore I came to deserve
much of that credit. There was no arguing against whatever dogmatic
declarations I made, but a quiet listening, an occasional question, and
sometimes an inspired commentary that cleared up not only the puzzle
I had pointed to, but a whole side of the play or the poem that I had not
understood. The teaching was being done by someone with the deepest
respect for text and poet, with the most careful and thorough reading and
rereading behind him, and with a great store of knowledge not only of
Shakespeare's plays but the history and society around and within them. I
had excellent teachers in grade school, in high school, in college, at Oxford
and at Yale, but this was a man, take him for all and all, I would not look
upon his like again.

Acknowledgments

Some of the poems in the present volume have also appeared in the journals *Massachusetts Review, Poetry East, Flyway, Nimrod, Anglistica, Elysium, Sun Tracks,* and *Epoch.* Others can be found in *Ponca War Dancers* (Point Riders Press, 1980), *Cowboys and Indians, Christmas Shopping* (Point Riders Press, 1992), or *An Eagle Nation* (University of Arizona Press, 1993). Versions of "Skins as Old Testament" and "What the Eagle Fan Says" appear in *Native American Songs and Poems* (ed. Brian Swann, Dover Thrift Publications, 1996). Others have not previously been published.

About the Author

Carter Revard, born in 1931 in the Osage Agency town of Pawhuska, Oklahoma, grew up in the Buck Creek Rural District on the Osage Reservation, twenty miles east of Pawhuska. Osage on his father's side, he was raised in a family that included his fullblood Osage stepfather and six mixed-blood brothers and sisters, as well as Ponca cousins, the children of his Uncle Woodrow Camp's Ponca wife, Jewell McDonald Camp. He graduated from the one-room Buck Creek School in 1944, then in 1948 from Bartlesville College High School, working—as described in the poems and prose of this book—at haying, harvesting, and training grey-hounds to help put food on the family table. As a senior in high school he competed on a radio quiz show and won a year's tuition scholarship to the University of Tulsa, where with support from scholarships and Professor Franklin Eikenberry, and working a hundred hours each month, he graduated with honors in 1952, was given a Rhodes Scholarship (Oklahoma and Merton, 1952), and went on to earn a B.A./M.A. from Oxford University and a Ph.D. from Yale University. His Osage grandmother arranged an Osage naming ceremony for him in September 1952, the highest honor he has received. He taught English and American Indian literature from 1956 to 1997, at Amherst College and at Washington University, St. Louis, and as a visiting professor at the University of Tulsa and University of Oklahoma. He retired in 1997 and lives in St. Louis. He has been a Gourd Dancer since 1977, and served from 1986 to 1997 as a board member of the American Indian Center of Mid-America in St. Louis.

His essays on medieval English and American Indian literature, and his poems, have appeared in numerous journals and anthologies. His books of poetry are *Ponca War Dancers* (1980), *Cowboys and Indians, Christmas Shopping* (1992), and *An Eagle Nation* (1993). A collection of his essays, *Family Matters, Tribal Affairs*, was published by the University of Arizona Press in 1998.